Nike

Nike

Tracy Carbasho

Foreword by Kelley Murray Skoloda

Corporations That Changed the World

 GREENWOOD

AN IMPRINT OF ABC-CLIO, LLC
Santa Barbara, California • Denver, Colorado • Oxford, England

Copyright 2010 by ABC-CLIO, LLC

Library of Congress Cataloging-in-Publication Data

Carbasho, Tracy.
    Nike / Tracy Carbasho ; foreword by Kelley Murray Skoloda.
        p. cm. — (Corporations that changed the world)
    Includes bibliographical references and index.
    ISBN 978-1-59884-342-2 (hard copy : alk. paper) — ISBN 978-1-
59884-343-9 (ebook) 1. Nike (Firm)—History. 2. Sporting goods
industry—United States—History. 3. Sports—United States—
Marketing. 4. Footwear industry—United States—History.
5. Athletic shoes—History. I. Title.
    HD9992.U54N553   2010
    338.7′68536—dc22   2010015774

ISBN: 978-1-59884-342-2
EISBN: 978-1-59884-343-9

14 13 12 11 10   1 2 3 4 5

This book is also available on the World Wide Web as an eBook.
Visit www.abc-clio.com for details.

Greenwood
An Imprint of ABC-CLIO, LLC

ABC-CLIO, LLC
130 Cremona Drive, P.O. Box 1911
Santa Barbara, California 93116-1911

This book is printed on acid-free paper ∞

Manufactured in the United States of America

My timeless love and gratitude to my brother Joe, my sister Jane, my other brother Tom Moroudas, and my best friend Mojo. Thank you for being the best family imaginable. In loving memory of my mother, Louise, my father, Pete, my brother Pete, and my precious Groucho.

Contents

Foreword

Our paths often intersect with other people's lives for a very profound purpose, even though we may not be aware of the reason at the time. That is the case with Tracy Carbasho, to whom I was introduced in late 2007 by a mutual colleague in the public relations field. At that time, I was looking for an editor for my book. After several conversations with Tracy, I realized she would provide a perfect combination of disciplined editing and enabling the book content to shine. That winning combination certainly rings true in this book about a company that has changed the world, Nike.

When you think about Nike, its business and its athletic affiliations, you think about prowess, speed, agility, business acumen, and a slogan that is recognized worldwide, "Just Do It." Well, I would use similar adjectives to capture what it takes to write a comprehensive book about Nike. To "Just Do It" when it comes to writing a book about this company is to embrace a daunting task, especially given the company's extensive history, its ever-changing innovation, and its affiliation with sometimes controversial big-name athletes. Tracy Carbasho has tackled the task with the skill of a professional.

Readers will be intrigued and discover everything they ever wanted to know about a company that, starting from humble beginnings, succeeded in making "Just Do It" the catch phrase of a generation. Tracy's interviews with top sports celebrities, such as Minnesota Vikings' running back Adrian Peterson and Phoenix Suns' guard Steve Nash, reveal compelling insights into why Nike has become legendary. Peterson and Nash share personal stories about their childhood dreams of wanting not only to excel in sports, but also to be like the heroes they watched as children in the Nike commercials. Today, they are now inspiring others as they live out their dream of having Nike on their side.

Dealing with athletes is not always a rosy business. Therefore, a book about Nike would not be complete without a chapter discussing the challenges that often occur when working with such Nike-sponsored athletes as Tiger Woods, Serena Williams, and Michael Vick. Tracy skillfully combines background information with vivid photos and colorful comments from industry leaders to demonstrate how the public's view of controversy surrounding their favorite athletes is not always the same as the sentiment expressed by Nike executives.

As a marketer, I found one of the most interesting aspects of the book to be the focus on Nike's communications—its advertising, marketing, and public relations. Creative, meaningful, and forceful communications have been a vital part of Nike's success and Tracy vividly paints images of the commercials and communications that have made Nike famous. Importantly, she then provides analytical information from several of the country's top advertising and marketing executives to show how and why these campaigns impacted the world.

Nike has always been known as an innovator in terms of constantly evolving its product technology to the next level. The technology seems to change so rapidly and so many new products are introduced each year that it is difficult to stay abreast of the latest announcements. However, Tracy has tracked the company's technology, financial results, and community outreach projects right down to the wire within days of meeting her publishing deadline to provide the most recent information.

This book is a must read not just for sports fans and history buffs, but also for business leaders, as well as advertising and marketing executives, who most certainly can learn lessons from Nike's success and who will benefit from the Nike examples. It is well written in a manner that makes you want to keep turning the pages, and it is chockfull of interesting photos of celebrities who are synonymous with Nike, including Peterson, Nash, Woods, Williams, Vick, Jordan, and more.

Just like Nike's founders were resourceful in keeping their dream alive, completing this project required a tremendous effort, a lot of heart, and immeasurable hours. The focus that was required to meet a tight deadline in the face of great personal adversity is a testament to Tracy's character. In fact, the commitment that fuels her work is similar to the passion that Nike co-founder Phil Knight feels for his company. Mark Lando, whose family founded The Athlete's Foot stores, tells a story in the book about Knight being so dedicated to doing company work that more than a year passed before he took the time to replace a shattered window in his Porsche.

That's dedication. That's what Tracy gives to all of us in this book.

Kelley Murray Skoloda
Author, *Too Busy to Shop*; and Partner, Ketchum

Acknowledgments

Losing sight of your dream is akin to gaining weight. Once your dream gets buried under a pile of other tasks on your "to do" list, it becomes a faint vision. The same thing occurs when you gain five pounds and fail to take action to lose the extra weight. Before long, you are 20 pounds heavier, and your former self is a distant memory.

Although I have been a professional writer for newspapers and magazines since I was in high school, I fell into the trap called adulthood. I was so busy earning a living as a newspaper writer just to pay the bills that I failed to see how many years were slipping away and I still had not written my own book. Well, actually, I wrote a romance novel when I was 21 years old, but I have never tried to market it. Perhaps that will be my next project.

I must thank Kelley Murray Skoloda, author of *Too Busy to Shop*, for finally lighting a fire under my feet. When Kelley asked me to edit her business book, I was so busy with my freelance writing career that I almost denied her request. Fortunately, I agreed and it was one of the best decisions I have ever made. Editing her work was an excellent motivator and reminded me once again of how much I wanted to write my own book. I owe Kelley my sincerest gratitude for motivating me, even though I'm sure she never realized what an impact she had on my life. I appreciate Tim O'Brien for putting me in touch with Kelley. Our collaboration was just the spark I needed to make the shift from writing newspaper articles to finally focusing on my book ideas.

It is not easy to complete a book while maintaining a busy schedule. However, I have a very supportive brother and sister who always try to make my hectic life a little easier, and care enough to leave me alone when I need space to work. All of my love to Jane and Joe for providing the space that was invaluable to the completion of this book. To my adopted brother Tom Moroudas, I love you just for being you. The three of you brighten my days and make it easier to look forward to tomorrow.

A special thank you must be extended to my friends, Penny, Doug, and Darcy Wright. You are a rare breed. Your unselfish kindness touched my heart more than you could ever imagine, renewing my faith in the goodness of people at a crucial time when I needed it the most. I cannot forget Jeannie Silveri for lending a helping hand when I was at my lowest, even though she had never met me.

I would have been lost without the unmatched friendship of Diana Jefferis, who has become the sister I never realized I had. Thank you for adding color to what was an otherwise dismal work environment. I deeply appreciate the constant encouragement and help of my friends Steve Lardis, Mike Sieber, and Dirk DeCoy. Steve has been helpful in my struggle to overcome roadblocks and Mike is a sweetheart who makes me laugh. Dirk helped me keep my "eyes on the prize" when writing this book, especially since there were so many distractions.

As the deadline loomed dangerously close, I was faced with unexpected health problems. Words almost fail me in attempting to thank Dr. Patsy Cipoletti for being the type of old-fashioned, caring doctor I used to see when I watched *Little House on the Prairie* as a kid. Thank you for honoring the oath you took to help your patients, being more knowledgeable than any doctor I have ever known, and having the compassion to listen.

I certainly cannot forget the people who made my book more interesting, especially Phoenix Suns' player Steve Nash and DC Headley, basketball communications manager for the Suns; Adrian Peterson from the Minnesota Vikings and Tom West, who made sure Adrian received my inquiry; Coach Mike Krzyzewski from Duke University and Jon Jackson, associate director of athletics/university and public affairs at Duke; Dean DeBiase, chairman of ReBoot Partners; Kenneth Halloy, president of Halloy Boy Sports Marketing, Inc.; and Mark Lando, owner of Arriba, Inc. Thank all of you for taking time from your hectic schedules to accommodate me. You are appreciated more than you will ever know.

Introduction

The word "Nike" has transcended its original definition in Greek mythology as the winged goddess of victory to become a household name. The victory part remains intact because the company that made the name Nike a hallmark is readily recognizable as the leader in its industry. In fact, Nike is well-known for many reasons in addition to being a top designer of athletic footwear, apparel, equipment, and accessories for numerous sports and fitness activities.

It is perhaps even better known for its association with the world's top-ranked athletes, some of whom have proven to be controversial. The most noteworthy athletes who helped the company generate impressive name recognition several decades ago were Michael Jordan, Bo Jackson, Deion Sanders, and John McEnroe. Back then, major controversy was seldom associated with the sports celebrities.

As new athletes have climbed to the top of their sport, Nike usually was on hand with an endorsement contract. For example, Tiger Woods was under contract to endorse Nike's products even before most people ever heard the golfer's name, proving the company knows a good thing when it sees it. Despite the scandal surrounding Woods in late 2009, he has still provided Nike with wonderful exposure by wearing the company's apparel even when he endorses products for other companies. In order to provide a comprehensive analysis of the impact that Woods and other celebrities have on the company, I conducted in-depth interviews with some of the country's top marketing and advertising executives. Their reaction to the manner in which Nike has addressed controversy stemming from the behavior of Woods, Michael Vick, and Serena Williams is compelling and informative.

Some marketing professionals believe Nike leaders are not opposed to controversy because it keeps the company's name in the spotlight. However, I believe the company has such a powerful arsenal of innovative technology, quality products, and dynamic advertising to its credit that unsolicited publicity is not necessary. Members of Nike's executive team apparently possess the same hunger for success that motivated co-founders Phil Knight and Bill Bowerman. They know when to maintain their affiliation with an athlete and when to cut their losses by moving on to sponsor the next up-and-coming star.

Young athletes, like Adrian Peterson of the Minnesota Vikings and LeBron James of the Cleveland Cavaliers, are attracted to the glory and glitz of the company because it was linked to the sports heroes they idolized as kids. Now, they are part of the Nike machine and proudly sport the famous "Swoosh" logo on their footwear and apparel. When gathering research for this book, I obtained comments from Peterson who shared his earliest memories of Nike. His remarks reveal the impact Nike had on him as a youngster and why he is so proud to endorse the company's products. I also talked to more seasoned professionals, such as Steve Nash from the Phoenix Suns, who is pleased Nike has taken a proactive stance by using environmentally friendly materials in its products.

Bowerman and Knight have been described as a bit eccentric. I think their quirkiness adds more life to the story about how they started the company from meager beginnings with nothing more than steadfast determination and a desire to win. Although their relentless drive rewarded them tenfold with an enormous return on investment, they have forged a company that believes in sharing the wealth—well, at least to a certain extent. The company collaborates with Tour de France legend Lance Armstrong each year to raise money for cancer research and recently embarked on an initiative to fight HIV/AIDS in Africa. Bono, the famed lead singer for the rock band U2, explains in the book why he wanted to partner with Nike on this charitable effort to combat AIDS.

Few people probably think of the winged goddess when they hear the word Nike today. The company has taken the name to such heights that it is easy to forget there ever was a winged goddess with the same name. Nike has been so embedded in our social consciousness that it would be easy to convince most people that Bowerman and Knight coined the word Nike.

The name is often synonymous with the phrase "Just Do It," the famous slogan from the 1980s that inspired generations to excel at sports and their life's work in general. It seems fitting that a company which invests so much time, money, and effort to create its products would have such a memorable catch phrase. Although other advertising taglines have been used over the years, this one is unmistakably the one that will forever be tantamount with Nike.

The company's story is inspiring for sports fans and even for individuals who get football confused with soccer. I hope you will find my version of the Nike story to be motivating enough to make you want to "Just Do It," no matter what "it" might be.

Chapter One

Inspiring Excellence

Adrian Peterson, the star running back for the Minnesota Vikings, wanted to be like the sports heroes he saw in the Nike commercials when he was a kid. Like so many athletes before him, he has achieved his dream. He provides interesting answers to my interview questions.

"Nike has influenced me a lot. I wanted to be like the guys in the Nike commercials—Bo, Deion, and Jordan," he recalls. "They were the guys I saw myself being as an athlete and I wanted to be like them when I grew up."

The commercials that inspired Peterson were generated by a company that started with a now infamous handshake which forever changed the look of the sports industry. That simple gesture of goodwill between two men who shared the same vision quickly evolved into NIKE, Inc., which has fueled the dreams of sports legends and backyard athletes for more than four decades.

Peterson was, of course, referring to professional sports icons Vincent Edward "Bo" Jackson, Deion Sanders, and Michael Jordan—all of whom were featured in Nike commercials at various times in the 1980s and 1990s. It made sense for companies to capitalize on the success of these particular athletes because they represented history in the making.

Sanders, who garnered the nickname Neon Deion in reverence to his flamboyant suits, is considered one of the all-time most versatile athletes in history because he played not only multiple sports, but also various positions. In 1989, he became the first player in history to hit a home run in Major League Baseball (MLB) and score a touchdown in the National Football League (NFL) in the same week.[1]

Following Sanders' first Super Bowl victory with the San Francisco 49ers in 1995, he hosted *Saturday Night Live*. He stretched his fame to the hilt and endorsed products for many companies, including Nike, Pepsi, Burger King, American Express, and Pizza Hut. In fact, he appeared in so many commercials that it is hard to remember any for being remarkable.

Adrian Peterson of the Minnesota Vikings takes a break on the sideline during the second quarter of an NFL game against the Seattle Seahawks in November 2009. (AP Photo/Hannah Foslien, File)

The commercials that Peterson remembers pertaining to Jackson and Jordan were far more memorable. I am sure an informal poll conducted on any street in the United States would result in many people readily remembering the Nike catch phrase "Bo Knows" and the vivid images of Jordan dunking unbelievable basketball shots for the Chicago Bulls. Several of the Jordan commercials, which featured the talent of high-profile producer Spike Lee, included the catch phrase "It's Gotta Be the Shoes."

The Nike "Bo Knows" advertisements, intended to promote a cross-training athletic shoe, paired Jackson and musician Bo Diddley. Although the commercials aired primarily in 1989 and 1990, you can still take a walk down memory lane by viewing them on YouTube™ (www.youtube.com). It was quite appropriate that Nike chose to have Jackson endorse its cross-training athletic shoe since he was the first athlete to be named an All-Star in both football and baseball.

Likewise, it is just as appropriate that Peterson's sports idols would include people like Jackson and National Basketball Association (NBA) superstar Jordan, whose incredible dunking power earned him the nickname Air Jordan. When I asked Peterson how old he was when he got his first pair of Nike shoes, he responded with one word: infant. His answer seemed a bit unlikely at first. However, it made more sense after I did some research and discovered that Nike introduced its first children's shoes in 1978, seven years before Peterson was born.

"I wanted to be a Nike athlete when I was little and I'm living out my dream now," says Peterson, who sports the No. 28 jersey for the Vikings.

Former San Francisco 49ers' cornerback Deion Sanders wears a Nike hat when he arrives for practice in Miami in 1998. (AP Photo/ Susan Ragan)

It is actually a bit uncanny that 1985 marked both the year that Peterson was born and the start of Jordan's affiliation with Nike. The first AIR JORDAN basketball shoe debuted that year and was endorsed by Jordan, who was just a rookie at the time. The original AIR JORDAN, which featured a red, white, and black color scheme with the famous Nike Swoosh emblem, was so revolutionary that it was banned by the NBA for violating its "uniformity of uniform" rule.[2]

Jordan's name has since become synonymous with Nike because he has endorsed the company's products for a quarter of a century. Twenty-three shoe designs were created with each subsequent one being given a new number starting with the original AIR JORDAN I all the way up to AIR JORDAN XX3, which went on the market in early 2008. Jordan Brand, a division of Nike, retired the labels AIR JORDAN I through XX3 in January 2009 and announced the creation of AIR JORDAN 2009. An even more high-tech shoe, called the AIR JORDAN 2010, was released in February of this year. The newest shoe

King of Pop Michael Jackson, who died in June 2009, fakes a football pass to his friend Bo Jackson of the Los Angeles Raiders and Kansas City Royals at Michael's recording studio in 1989. (AP Photo/Kevork Djansezian)

features a revolutionary design with a layered-toe construction that has an independent forefoot support cover. The shoe enables athletes to be more agile because it actually replicates the flexibility and movement of their feet.

"With each shoe, consumers have pushed me to take the next AIR JORDAN beyond their wildest imagination," says Jordan. "The AIR JORDAN 2010 marks the future of the Jordan Brand and proves there are no limits to what this brand is capable of creating."[3]

It's no wonder that Peterson uses the word "innovative" to describe Nike and "inspirational" to characterize the company's commercials. One of Jordan's most memorable commercials is also one of my favorites. I believe the "failure" commercial, which can readily be located and viewed on the Internet, is extremely well written with a positive message. You would not expect a spot that talks about failures to be the least bit motivating, but it is. Trust me.

The commercial shows Jordan walking through a room and you can hear him talking about the pitfalls he has suffered on the court. In particular, he mentions missing more than 9,000 shots in his career and failing after being trusted 26 times to make the game-winning shot. At the end of the commercial, Jordan exits through a door as you hear his final message: "I've failed over and over in my life and that's why I succeed."

That ranks as one of the most inspirational messages I have ever encountered in any type of marketing. I suppose the message might

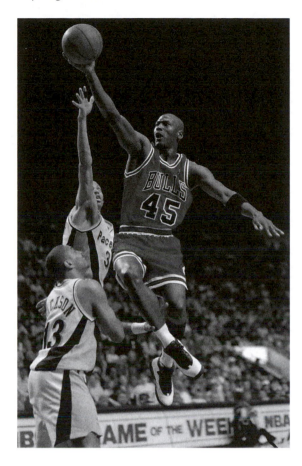

Chicago Bulls' guard Michael Jordan soars to the hoop over the Pacers' Reggie Miller and Mark Jackson during a game in Indianapolis in 1995. (AP Photo/Michael Conroy)

be lost on some viewers, but I think it speaks volumes about the need to keep trying new things each day and to continually pursue our dreams—even in the face of challenges and setbacks.

Peterson, who now stars in his own Nike commercials, explains,

The images in the commercials are inspirational and they were to me even when I was younger. Nike makes everyone feel like an athlete. The shoes and clothes started a whole new lifestyle trend among people of all walks of life. I hope young people look up to me in the commercials.

Peterson is featured in several Nike commercials that are no doubt both interesting and inspiring for youths and adults. One simply shows a series of still pictures of him in his Vikings uniform and at the end, the words "Just Do It" appear on the screen followed by Nike's signature Swoosh logo. The company obviously opted to resurrect its "Just Do It" slogan, which is now ensconced in U.S. history with an official place in the Smithsonian Institution in Washington, D.C. We will discuss the company's unforgettable advertising campaigns in a later chapter. I will also share interview responses from other major sports celebrities, including Steve Nash from the Phoenix Suns, and top collegiate coaches, such as Mike Krzyzewski from Duke University. For now, let's return to Peterson.

A second commercial celebrates Peterson being named Rookie of the Year in 2007. I just saw the commercial recently when I searched for it on YouTube and it definitely meets Nike's standards of producing quality marketing materials. Peterson's voice can be heard as he explains how his goals in life included winning the Rookie of the Year honor. "When you set the bar like that, you work hard and anything is possible," he states in the commercial, which shows him going the extra mile with his physical fitness training program. These words are flashed on the screen as you see him training: "One more step, one more rep, one more goal achieved."

As for the future, Peterson has set a few more goals for himself. "I want to help the Vikings win a Super Bowl, grow my relationship with Nike, keep winning games, and be a better man every day."

Peterson's attitude about continually improving his game and his life is similar to the philosophy that has kept Nike at the top of the athletic footwear industry since 1964. In order to explore the magnitude of what the company has achieved, we must first look back to see where the story began. It might surprise you to learn that the forerunner to what eventually became known as the Nike athletic shoes actually were sold by one of the founders from the trunk of his Plymouth Valiant. From these humble beginnings sprang a dynasty.

Chapter Two

The Vision behind the Victory

Never let it be said that greatness cannot be built upon a modest foundation. Nike is a shining example of the results that can be achieved when a dream is bolstered by determination, perseverance, creativity, resourcefulness, and a lot of old-fashioned sweat.

The men who invested long hours and plenty of ingenuity to spin their dream into a reality were Bill Bowerman, a renowned track and field coach at the University of Oregon; and Phil Knight, a talented runner who competed for the University of Oregon's track team.[1]

Bowerman, who was a nationally respected coach, was just as recognized for his persistence in trying to give a competitive advantage to the athletes in his program. He truly believed "if you have a body, you are an athlete." It's a simple, understated observation, but his company later made millions of people throughout the world feel as if they were every bit as fast, agile, and powerful as the athletes who endorse Nike products.

According to the company history described on www.nikebiz.com, Bowerman "experimented with different track surfaces, re-hydration drinks, and most importantly—innovations in running shoes."

When the established footwear manufacturers of the 1950s snubbed his ideas, Bowerman began cobbling his own shoes for the runners. He was obviously a man who believed strongly in his ideas and was not deterred by the rejection from existing shoe manufacturers. Imagine how dejected the manufacturers must have felt years later when they realized they had missed an exciting opportunity to be part of something spectacular.

While Bowerman was trying to design better shoes for his track and field athletes, Knight was working on ideas of his own that also pertained to manufacturing high-quality running shoes. Being a middle-distance runner, he definitely could lend a first-hand perspective to the art of creating better athletic footwear. After graduating from the University of Oregon, he went on to earn his Master's in Business Administration from Stanford University. While attending

Stanford in 1962, he wrote a paper explaining how low-priced, high-performance running shoes manufactured in Japan could topple the domination of German manufacturers selling to U.S. markets.[2] I would not say that Knight encountered the same rejection that Bowerman had experienced at the hands of manufacturers. Rather, he was simply ignored because manufacturers in Japan and Asia did not respond to his letters.

Bowerman and Knight apparently had more in common than just the University of Oregon and a desire to create better shoes. They were kindred spirits in terms of their unwavering willpower. Knight could have moved on to another adventure in life after failing to receive a response from the overseas manufacturers, but he chose a more difficult option. The path he selected ultimately reunited him with his former track coach, and spawned the infamous handshake that finally set their dreams into motion.

Knight took a chance by visiting the Onitsuka Tiger Co., a company based in Kobe, Japan, that manufactured high-quality athletic shoes. He convinced the company to let him be a distributor for the Tiger shoes in the United States. When he received the first shipment of samples, he sent several pairs to Bowerman in hopes of making an initial sale. What he received, however, was far better and somewhat unexpected.

Bowerman, who took over as the head track coach at the university in 1948, was pleased with the samples and made Knight a proposal he could not refuse. He offered to become Knight's partner and to lend his own design ideas to the Tiger shoes. And as the old saying goes, the rest is history. In 1964, the men formed Blue Ribbon Sports (BRS), the precursor to Nike, by shaking hands and each committing to proffer $500 in start-up capital. Their first business task was to place an order for 300 pairs of Tiger shoes, which Knight peddled from his father's basement and the back of his car. The first shipment sold out in just three weeks. At the same time, Bowerman was dissecting the Tiger shoes to discover ways to make them lighter, and then letting his track runners test his creations.

Ask anyone who has read about the history of Nike and they will point to Bowerman and Knight as the founders. True, they were the brains and brawn who spurred the genesis of the company. However, Jeff Johnson played an extremely instrumental role in Nike's creation, although his name is not as readily associated with the company. It was clear that the two founders could not do all of the work that was necessary to keep the young company moving forward, especially since Bowerman was the head track coach and Knight was working as an accountant. Then in 1965, along came Johnson, who was also a runner at Stanford.

Working on commission as the first employee of BRS, Johnson was skilled at multi-tasking long before the word was ever fashionable in corporate America. The Nike archives reveal that Johnson developed the first marketing materials for the company, took photographs for the catalogs, established a mail-order system, managed the shipping and receiving functions, opened the first BRS retail store in Santa Monica, California, and even designed a few early shoe models.

Yet one of his biggest contributions would come from a dream he had in 1971, which turned out to be the beginning of a productive decade for the company. The stakeholders at BRS believed Johnson's dream about Nike, the Greek goddess of victory, was more than just a strange nighttime blur. They decided that "The Nike" would be the name for the company's first soccer cleat that featured the now famous Swoosh logo. Knight's notion of calling the new shoe "Dimension 6" was shot down in favor of the name that stemmed from Johnson's for-tuitous dream. A t-shirt promoting the new shoe, which was manufac-tured in Mexico, hit the market as the company's first apparel item.[3]

The Swoosh logo, which is quickly identified throughout the world today as Nike's trademark, represents the wing of the Greek goddess that appeared in Johnson's dream. The famous logo was created by Portland State University graphic design student Carolyn Davidson, who continued working for Nike until 1983.[4] She charged the company $35 for her services, a small price to pay for a design that has with-stood the test of time, adorned the apparel of thousands of top ath-letes, and become one of the most recognized marks in the world. Knight's initial reaction to the creation was, "I don't love it, but it will grow on me." When Davidson retired, Knight presented her with a diamond ring engraved with the Swoosh logo and an undisclosed amount of stock in the company.[5] Perhaps the logo did, indeed, grow on him over the years.

With the affiliation between BRS and Onitsuka Tiger Co. deterio-rating around 1972, it seemed like the perfect time for the founders to start doing what they wanted to do from the beginning—design and manufacture their own brand of athletic shoes. All of the pieces were coming together, but not by chance or accident. The company was moving in the right direction because the powers-that-be were care-fully planning each step and strategically plotting their next move.

Bowerman was so inventive that one of his designs in the early 1970s was based on experiments he conducted using his wife's waffle iron. The idea for the new shoes, which featured an outsole with light-weight waffle-type nubs for traction, was generated by pouring a liquid rubber compound into the waffle iron. This particular sole changed the design of running shoes forever and I'm sure his wife was happy to sacrifice her waffle iron for the good of the company.

BRS launched its Nike footwear at the National Sporting Goods Show in Chicago in 1972 and received a positive response from retailers. A year later, Romanian tennis idol Ilie Nastase became the first professional athlete to sign an endorsement contract with BRS.[6] In

1973, the young American record holder Steve Prefontaine earned the title of the first major track athlete to wear the Nike brand shoes. The 1970s kept getting better for BRS as the waffle shoe topped the list as the best-selling training shoe in the nation.

Mark Lando, former owner of The Athlete's Foot Marketing Associates, Inc., has first-hand knowledge about Nike's climb to the top based on what he witnessed in the industry. His uncle David opened the first location of The Athlete's Foot in Pittsburgh in 1972. He recalls that at the time this particular store opened, Converse and Adidas dominated the athletic footwear industry. Converse has since been purchased by Nike and is now a wholly owned subsidiary.

Lando attributes the company's growing presence as a full-line manufacturer, rather than just a running company, to a strike that prevented Adidas from shipping basketball shoes to the United States. He believes this incident carved out the perfect opportunity for Nike to make its move and capture more of the market.

"Nike always wanted to appeal to the masses and that's why the company has always made so many different shoes," says Lando, who now owns the Arriba, Inc. franchise and specialty retail consulting company in Pittsburgh. "Nike is known for its creativity and innovation, but the company was never known for having the absolute top-quality shoes."

Instead, he believes that spot would now be reserved for New Balance, an American company that established its niche as the only athletic footwear manufacturer that produced top-quality shoes in various widths, giving the customer a unique fit experience; and Asics, a Japanese company that started as the leader in the wrestling shoe market, but now is known for its running shoes.

Lando and his father purchased the franchise rights to The Athlete's Foot in 1975 and changed the incorporated name of the company to The Athlete's Foot Marketing Associates, Inc. Back then, there were 12 stores. However, their aggressive franchise marketing strategy led to the development of more than 50 stores within just one year.

Meanwhile, BRS was rapidly becoming a trailblazer in its own right in the athletic shoe industry and eventually changed its name to Nike in 1978. The company signed the larger-than-life tennis pro John McEnroe to endorse its products. It was a complementary fit because McEnroe's persona was as vibrant as Nike's growing popularity. Both the man and the company were on the verge of becoming household names.

By the time Lando and his father sold the Athlete's Foot Marketing Associates in 1984, the company had grown to include 475 stores worldwide and the sale of Nike shoes accounted for more than 60 percent of the annual revenue. Lando put the percentage into perspective by noting that the average Athlete's Foot location was doing approximately $750,000 in annual volume at that point. If you multiply that revenue by 475 stores, you get a very large number. I never enjoyed math and I'm not going to grab a calculator, but you can clearly see why Nike's influence was so strong.

Lando learned lessons from indirectly working with Nike that he later used in his business career. He stresses that once Nike became powerful, the company attempted to bully vendors into purchasing its products. However, he notes that no multi-brand shoe retailer wants 60 or 70 percent of its business to come from the same vendor for fear that a strike or a simple disagreement could spell trouble. He explains,

> In the 1980s, there was a concerted effort to drive more of our business to other vendors. The lesson here for Nike is to never forget where you came from. Nike became the No. 1 most recognized brand and logo in the world over Coca-Cola and it clearly was the result of branding. They've always had good products and controversial products that provide a unique look and they've pushed the envelope. They knew they could succeed because they had a youth following that would do anything to get a pair of Nike shoes. I remember the news stories about kids beating each other up in school just to steal their Nike shoes.

Lando remembers plenty of pleasant stories about his association with the personalities at Nike. He told me an amusing story about Knight that will forever stay with me, especially when I start to lose sight of my own important projects. He had no qualms about saying that Nike leaders are just as colorful and bold as some of the company's shoes. His recollection is that when Knight briefly left the company, sales dipped and performance suffered. Fortunately, when he returned, the company pulled out of the doldrums and again became the formidable leader in the industry. Knight resigned as chief executive officer (CEO) in 2004 but continues to serve as chairman.

Lando recalls the following about Knight:

> I'll always remember one story about Phil Knight when we attended an event together in Beaverton, Oregon. He picked me up in an old Porsche and the back window had been broken out and replaced with plastic. I noticed there was still a lot of shattered glass on the back seat, so I asked him what happened. He replied that someone broke the window out to try to get into the car. Knight is wealthy and he's equally as eccentric. I thought the glass had been broken recently, but he said it had occurred more than a year ago and that he never had time to get it repaired. He was a man on a mission and he did not do things that were not important to his particular focus at a given time.

That steadfast focus paid off with major dividends for Knight, Bowerman, and the company in general. Before long, athletes participating in major sports throughout the world were competing while wearing Nike shoes. British runner Steve Ovett was the first athlete to win an Olympic medal while wearing the Swoosh-bearing footwear at the 1980 games in Moscow.[7] As a side note, the best distance runners from the United States did not compete in the 1980 Summer Olympics because of a boycott that was staged by many countries to protest the Soviet war in Afghanistan. It is hard to say who might have stood on the platform to receive medals had President Jimmy Carter not issued the boycott. Joining the United States in the boycott were West Germany, Canada, Japan, and China.

Nike's relationship with China flourished in 1980 when the company began negotiations to have its athletic shoes produced in this Far East country. The next year, the company started promoting its products in China by supplying the men's and women's national basketball teams with shoes and apparel.[8] The company continued to expand its global presence by opening its first European headquarters in Amsterdam, the Netherlands, in 1981.

With global momentum that was as fast-paced as some of the sports heroes who were wearing their shoes and apparel, Nike officials knew it was time to turn up the heat against any would-be competitors. They started to aggressively promote their products by building on the company's early tagline of "There is no finish line." These words, which were featured in a 1977 advertisement, were more than just the components of a gimmicky sales pitch. A special history section on the company's Web site states, "If there is any way to describe the fire of a true competitor or the internal ethos of Nike, it was the tagline for this 1977 ad, which became Nike's first poster."

While the two Nike founders were seeing their dream come alive in vivid color with soaring sales, two other men were joining forces to create their own company. As fate would have it, these men—Dan Wieden and David Kennedy—would provide the creative spark for Nike's most memorable advertising campaigns.

The advertising agency started in Oregon by Wieden and Kennedy in 1982 is now one of the largest independently owned firms in the world. The agency, called Wieden+Kennedy, readily gained prominence and a string of big-name clients after uttering those three little words, "Just Do It," that catapulted Nike into the history books for its innovative advertising campaigns. In 2007, the firm, whose client list also includes Coca-Cola and Levi's, was named Global Agency of the Year by *AdWeek*.

Before Wieden+Kennedy's brainstorming led to those three iconic words, Knight apparently had three words of his own for Wieden: "I hate advertising."[9]

Chapter Three

Just Do It

Perhaps Knight was not crazy about advertising in the beginning, but it must have become rapidly apparent to him that one of the best ways to promote the company's products was to "just do it." And that is precisely what the company has done since the beginning by advertising with increasingly powerful, full-blown campaigns.

My all-time favorite commercial merges time and technology to bring together the 2008 U.S. Men's Olympic Basketball Team and one-of-a-kind recording artist Marvin Gaye more than two decades after Gaye's death. The commercial captures a celebrated moment in time when Gaye performed a poignant rendition of "The Star Spangled Banner" at the 1983 NBA All Star Game. The spot features clips of Gaye singing while members of the gold medal-winning team do what they do best on the court. A close-up shot spotlights the Nike shoes being worn by the players and the fabulous commercial ends perfectly by resurrecting the words "Just Do It" on the screen.

This will always be my favorite commercial by any company because it is inspirational and includes one of my favorite singers. Of course, when Gaye performed the song in 1983, I was only a teenager. Therefore, his version of the national anthem, using only a drum machine for accompaniment, did not come to my attention until a few years ago when I realized what a magnificent talent he was.

Nike's advertisements are known for featuring magnificent talent, whether it is in the form of the athletes who are in the spotlight or the creative designers who develop such memorable campaigns. The commercials have consistently championed a motivational message and have changed over the years to reflect the most up-to-date methods of reaching consumers.

"The strength of Nike's campaigns is that the company has always understood what it is as a brand and understood in a holistic sense who its customer is," notes Dean DeBiase, chairman of Reboot Partners in Lake Forest, Illinois. "It is a strategy that was developed at the brand's inception in 1978 and that it has had the discipline and vision to remain faithful to, even as its marketing strategy has evolved over the decades."

I was more than happy when DeBiase agreed to provide comments for my book. He is a nationally recognized expert in advertising and brand strategy. He has served as the CEO of a variety of public and private companies, including TNS Media, which is a leading advertising, entertainment, digital engagement, and social media research analytics company. He was also CEO of The Imagination Network, a social media games company that was acquired by AOL and ranked by comScore Media Metrix as "the No. 1 games destination in cyberspace."

DeBiase, co-author of *The Big Moo: Stop Trying to Be Perfect and Start Being Remarkable*, has a reputation for building global consumer and business services companies in not only advertising and media, but also in technology, entertainment, and Internet industries. He has led private and public companies through turnarounds, divestitures, expansions, mergers and acquisitions, as well as Initial Public Offering growth phases. As a result of his extensive and impressive curriculum vitae, he is a preferred speaker at engagements throughout the country. *The Big Moo*, published by Penguin Books in 2005, is a compilation of stories from 33 business leaders who discuss strategies for customer service, leadership, and company innovation in general.

Today, DeBiase is working hard as the chairman of Reboot Partners, a global growth management and board advisement group that helps organizations address their most challenging issues, seize market opportunities, and motivate people to deliver the next generation of innovation and tangible business results.

Over the years, he has closely followed Nike's rise to power in the athletic shoe industry and has plenty to say about the company's advertising efforts. He explains,

> Before it started advertising in 1982, Nike concentrated on sponsorships and endorsements of both professional athletes and college teams. This provided the brand with not only a core constituency that helped validate its authenticity as footwear specifically designed for athletes, but it also provided unique insight into the emotional motivation and makeup of athletes. Nike has always positioned itself as the essence of what drives the athletes and those who want to be more active, and uniquely understands the emotional motivation and reward of doing so. Its "Just Do It" campaign epitomizes this. It embodies both the exhilaration and the challenges of competition and fitness. It speaks directly to the emotions of athletes.

DeBiase says the "Just Do It" campaign in 1988 was the first Nike advertising effort that really captured his attention. He is far from alone in his opinion that the motivational message extends beyond sports. He believes:

> It is a prime example that if you want to build a true community, advertising has to be about the consumers you serve, not just about the brand. This is how you drive ownership of a brand and build advocates. Nike is a model for what all brands should become. It's not just about selling product. It's about building an environment upon a brand essence that actually contributes to and enhances the consumer's life. It offers reciprocal value to the consumer's life in return for the attention that the consumer provides to their promotions. You always come away from interaction with the brand with a benefit, with something that has enhanced your life.

The 1980s started off with a bang for the company, which by this time had become a publicly traded entity and had unveiled its successful Nike Air technology in the Tailwind running shoe. By the mid-1980s, however, the word "tailspin" would have been a more accurate way to describe what was occurring at Nike. According to the company's historical data,

> Nike had slipped from its position as the industry leader in part because the company had badly miscalculated on the aerobics boom, giving upstart competitors an almost completely open field to develop the business. Fortunately, the debut of a new signature shoe for an NBA rookie by the name of Michael Jordan in 1985 helped bolster Nike's bottom line.

The company also took action in 1987 to regain its industry position by unleashing a major marketing campaign to promote Air Max, the first footwear to showcase the innovative Nike Air cushioning system. Before the "Just Do It" commercials began enhancing people's lives with a motivational slant, another Nike advertising campaign highlighted a television commercial with the soundtrack of the Beatles' hit "Revolution." It was no coincidence that this song was selected as the backdrop to a campaign that was built on the revolutionary Air Max. The "Just Do It" tagline appeared the following year.

Brilliant advertising continued to play a pivotal role in Nike's industry position throughout the remainder of the decade with the "Bo Knows" campaigns hitting the screen in 1989. These particular advertisements coincided with an increase in the company's cross-training business, capitalizing on Bo Jackson's excellence in football and baseball.

Numerous top-name players in football, baseball, basketball, tennis, soccer, golf, track, and cycling have donned Nike footwear since

Bo Jackson takes his turn
at bat for the Kansas City
Royals in 1989. (AP Photo)

the 1980s. The faces have changed from Michael Jordan and Bo Jackson
to Kobe Bryant, Tiger Woods, Adrian Peterson, Steve Nash, and countless others. Just as the faces have changed to include today's popular
sports professionals, the messages have evolved to be consistent with
the times.

The company garnered Emmy Awards for its "Morning After"
and "Move" television ads, which appeared in 2000 and 2002, respec-
tively. The "Morning After" spot was a spoof of the Y2K hysteria that
was occurring at the time. It showed a man jogging on January 1, 2000,
passing by various scenes where anything that could have gone wrong at
the start of the new millennium apparently did. "Move" featured athletic
movements that continued with fluidity from one sport to another.

DeBiase observes:

> Its entire being as a brand is to listen closely to and mirror what
> is happening and emerging on a grassroots level. This has

served the brand well in terms of the direction of its creativity, and it has done an excellent job of evolving and driving advertising trends. Nike was also a pioneer in identifying sports and athletes/athletic wear as a fashion statement because of its closeness to the grassroots. This is what gave it an important competitive advantage over Reebok. It recognized the emergence of sports as a lifestyle, embraced it, and drove the trend.

He emphasizes that Nike has always driven new trends, but the company has remained faithful to its brand identity and has never forgotten that a brand's power is derived from its customers. The brand never tries to dictate to the customers.

A prime example of Nike driving advertising trends was the campaign launched in 2005 to target women and their so-called celebrated body parts, such as their "thunder thighs," according to DeBiase. It celebrated the diversity of women's anatomy, especially those of athletes, much in the same way that Dove's Campaign for Real Beauty did.

Kelley Murray Skoloda, another powerhouse in the global advertising arena, agrees that the marketing campaigns associated with Nike have been effective, bold, and creative. However, she also believes the company has catered primarily to the male audience, despite having several initiatives and campaigns that feature women.

"I remember some of the first 'Just Do It' ads and how powerful and empowering they appeared. They made you feel like you could and should do anything you wanted," she recalls. "I also remember feeling like they were talking to men and not directly to me as a woman who also felt that same power and desire to accomplish."

Skoloda, a partner/director at the Pennsylvania-based Ketchum's Global Brand Marketing Practice, is a nationally recognized authority on marketing to women. She is the author of the bestselling book, *Too Busy to Shop: Marketing to Multi-Minding Women*, which provides insight about proven advertising methods to effectively reach the female audience. Her work has been featured in *BusinessWeek Online*, the *Washington Post*, *BRANDWEEK*, *CNNMoney.com*, and many other publications. Skoloda is *the* true marketing authority when it comes to capturing a busy woman's attention. She points out:

Nike has had an impact because the company empowered people before it was en vogue to be empowered. They led a trend, a movement, to do what you want to the best of your ability. They also sponsor the *best of the best* athletes, bringing that empowerment to life for all to see across almost every sport today. They walk their talk, which is extremely important in this day of authenticity.

Even though Skoloda believes Nike's campaigns have been effective, she thinks the company could do more to capture the attention of the female audience. She explains:

> The bold approach with sports images and few words resonates strongly with the male audience. With women being a key buyer of athletic gear for themselves and their families, effectively connecting with women is an area in which Nike could improve. There have been a few, well done campaigns, but I am surprised that they have not expanded their approach to be more appealing to women overall.

Skoloda points to several companies that are doing a good job of targeting the female audience. Harley-Davidson, for instance, is educating women about motorcycles, making the showroom experience more female-friendly, adding more color to its clothing, and producing bikes that are more comfortable for women.

In Skoloda's book, she cites statistics that clearly show the ever-increasing buying power of women. For example, women now control $3.3 trillion in consumer spending, are responsible for more than 80 percent of the household buying, control more than 50 percent of the wealth in the country, make 62 percent of all car purchases, and take more than 50 percent of all business trips.

Given these statistics, more and more companies are heeding Skoloda's advice by providing useful information in a meaningful and quick way that does not interrupt a woman's busy day. Instead, the messages are delivered in a manner that builds trust in the company by providing information that women can use to make their days less hectic. Many companies are using Web sites that feature comments from other product users to help build relationships with their customers and this method seems to be working. Skoloda states in her book,

> Consistent online efforts, local marketing events, consumer panels, key blogger relationships, partnerships with social networking sites, and other vehicles that enable you to forge a real relationship with your female consumers is crucial. Social networking sites, enabling users to automatically make recommendations and endorsements through purchase confirmations, will become that river of trusted information.

TAKING STRIDES TOWARD DIVERSITY

Perhaps Nike has realized the need to pay more attention to its female audience and to be more diverse in general. In March 2009, the company launched the Nike Challenge: "Men vs. Women," a virtual running race on www.nikeplus.com. We will discuss the technological innovation behind Nike+ later, but I will give you a brief description here to help you understand the race.

Nike+, launched in 2006, enables Nike+ running shoes to send data wirelessly to a Nike+ SportBand, an iPod nano, or an iPod touch. The information includes data on distance, pace, time, and calories burned. Participating runners can establish goals, challenge others to virtual competitions, connect with friends, and obtain valuable advice from the Nike+Coach component.

The special "Men vs. Women" campaign included a television commercial with appearances by athletes Roger Federer, Zlatan Ibrahimovic, Tony Parker, Eva Longoria Parker, Paula Radcliffe, Sofia Boutella, and Fernando Torres. Each celebrity described his or her perspective on the rivalry between men and women.

"Women are generally better organized and more consistent," says Radcliffe, a marathon world record holder. "You might see the guys start off a bit faster and probably running at a quicker pace, but they're fair-weather runners. If the rain or snow comes in, the guys are going to bottle out."[1]

However, the men have a different opinion. "Men are better competitors," says Inter Milan striker Ibrahimovic. "We're more powerful and, mentally, we're tougher."[2]

Friendly competition is always a good way to show sportsmanship and to bolster one's own athletic confidence. The inspiration for this Nike event came directly from a consumer who posted the challenge on the nikeplus.com site.

Nike also sponsors an annual Women's Marathon, the largest race of its kind in the world, to raise awareness and money for the Leukemia & Lymphoma Society (LLS). More than $14 million was raised in the October 2009 event, which attracted in excess of 20,000 participants from throughout the United States and 25 foreign countries. The event, which was started in 2004, is held in San Francisco.

"It's a race that is very dear to my heart and I am so proud to support it," says Joan Benoit Samuelson, former Olympian who served as the inspiration for the event. "The Nike Women's Marathon is an amazing event that inspires thousands of women from all over the world to run for themselves and a great cause."[3]

According to Nike's media site, the marathon was started to commemorate the 20th anniversary of Samuelson's gold-medal victory in the inaugural women's marathon at the 1984 Olympics in Los Angeles. Since then, more than 80,000 women have laced up their running shoes to participate and more than $92 million has been raised.

"The Nike Women's Marathon is a celebration of women coming together to enjoy a shared experience," says Nancy Klein, chief marketing and revenue officer for the LLS. "It is always so inspiring to see so many women working hard to reach that finish line, while also making a difference in the lives of thousands of people fighting blood cancer."[4]

Amy White, vice president of running for Nike, North America, describes the race as a celebration of the company's support for female athletes. "It's one of our shining examples of how we're enriching the lives of women through the power of sport."[5]

The marathon offers numerous activities that cater to women with the underlying concept that their running life has two aspects: lifestyle and athleticism. Special activities at the 2009 event included course preview talks, advice on nutrition, a photo booth, an oxygen bar, massages, manicures, and presentations by Samuelson and world-class marathon runner Kara Goucher. Nike women's apparel was also available for purchase.

Nike has a diversity and inclusion component built into its organizational structure. The purpose is not to just include more women, but also to ensure that the company's makeup of more than 30,000 employees includes people of diverse backgrounds and skill sets.

Gina Warren heads this particular effort in her capacity as vice president of global diversity and inclusion. "Diversity and inclusion are fundamental to Nike's performance. It's what makes us better. It's what makes us smarter. It's what helps our business grow and helps us connect with consumers."[6]

A special Diversity and Inclusion Team is responsible for engaging employees, providing business consultation, and developing innovative tools, models, and designs. In order to achieve true diversity among its employees, the company has developed the following strategy:

- Cultivate diversity and inclusion to develop world-class, high-performing teams
- Ignite change and inspire critical conversations around diversity, inclusion, and innovation
- Create venues and environments for open dialogue, diverse opinions, and a multitude of perspectives

The strategy is intended to drive the recruitment of dynamic employees; enrich the creativity and innovation that shapes the brand; enhance the company's competitive advantage; and improve the stature of the brand.

At the same time Nike has been trying to pay more attention to female customers, it also has been focusing on the most innovative methods of reaching all consumers, male and female. The answer was found in the use of social media, such as Twitter™, blogging, Facebook™, and other networking sites.

ENGAGING CUSTOMERS VIA SOCIAL MEDIA

Skoloda gives Nike a good grade for its brilliant use of social media, which is permeating the communications of many brands and businesses as consumers demand enhanced engagement with their favorite companies.

Nike has emerged as a leader in using social media to connect with consumers. With its own YouTube channel, blog, Twitter handle, and Facebook activities, Nike has been active in the social media space.

In fact, the ENGAGEMENTdb Report, a study conducted to measure the financial value of social media, lists Nike as number seven among 100 brands in regard to social media performance. Completed by the Altimeter Group and Wetpaint, the study is based on the world's 100 most valuable brands that are widely recognized for setting the standards in marketing as measured by the *BusinessWeek/Interbrand Best Global Brands 2008* rankings. The results, which were released in July 2009, can be viewed at www.engagementdb.com.[7]

The findings reveal positive financial results for companies that have the greatest social media engagement. As part of the study, more than 10 social media channels, including blogs, Facebook, Twitter, wikis, and discussion forums, were reviewed. The activity in each channel was then ranked based on the amount of interaction with scores for brand engagement ranging from a high of 127 to a low of just one.

The top 10 companies that are actively engaging their customers via social media, according to the study, are as follows:

1. Starbucks (127)
2. Dell (123)
3. eBay (115)
4. Google (105)
5. Microsoft (103)
6. Thomson Reuters (101)
7. Nike (100)
8. Amazon (88)
9. SAP (86)
10. Tie: Yahoo! and Intel (85)

A press release issued by Wetpaint states:

Companies that scored well in the study generally have dedicated teams, however small, active in the social media channels they utilize. The study found that the most successful teams evangelize social media across the entire organization to pull in a broad range of stakeholders. These companies view social media as an indispensable tool to help them achieve results, and their approach is conversational.

"This is the first study of this depth on the top global brands and we think the results provide a good guide for corporations and brand marketers in every industry," says Charlene Li, founder of the San Mateo, California-based Altimeter Group. "The success stories we have uncovered provide a blueprint for companies making decisions about how to best apply their marketing and consumer relations resources."[8]

The Altimeter Group provides thought leadership, research, and consulting on digital strategies. It was founded in 2008 by Li, a veteran technology and business analyst and co-author of the bestselling business book, *Groundswell: Living in a World Transformed by Social Technologies*.

Ben Elowitz, CEO of Wetpaint, the consumer-friendly wiki for online publishing and collaboration, states in a press release that the study goes a long way toward validating the importance of social media for business. In particular, he notes the closer any company is to its customers, the better, and it is hard to argue with the ability for social media to create such proximity. "In this day and age, companies should feel much more comfortable investing in social media—the correlation to results is so clear."

DeBiase, who gave his opinion on Nike's marketing campaigns earlier in this chapter, also commented on the company's use of social media. His input and the ranking received by the company in the ENGAGEMENTdb study clearly point to a business that is serious about interacting with customers.

"Nike has been a very aggressive user of social media, inherently understanding that this platform is more about engagement than purely building brand awareness," he says. "A recent example is its *Back Your Block* campaign, whereby the company offered $650,000 in grants to neighborhood groups that use sports programs as a tool to change the community."

Groups can apply online at www.nikebackyourblock.com and then use Facebook and Twitter to encourage people to vote for their organization.

The NikePlus (also known as Nike+) site is a good example of how companies can use social marketing to their advantage and help customers at the same time. The site can be accessed at http://nikerunning.com/nikeos/p/nikeplus/en_US/. The site represents the July 2009 merger of NikePlus.com with NikeRunning.com. It also includes NikeiD, a special section where visitors can customize shoes and apparel to a certain extent.

DeBiase believes the site was conceived to bring runners together and to sell them the $29 Sport Kit sensor. "As a result of community interest among runners, Nike has sold 1.3 million Nike+ iPod Sports Kits and a half million SportBands at $59 a pop. Total sales were $56 million in 2008, which is just a drop in the sales bucket for Nike, but an important community for the company, nonetheless."

Nike's running site is chockfull of information and helpful tips for runners, meaning the average person who runs on a regular basis as opposed to professional athletes. In this way, the company is connecting to its most valuable resource, its customers. Individuals can use their Nike+ iPod or SportBand, both of which include special sensors, to track their distance, pace, time, and calories burned. This information can be used to set goals and track accomplishments on the site. Visitors can also challenge others to virtual races, connect with friends, and benefit from using the Nike+Coach special feature.

"We're giving runners a seamless, comprehensive, one-stop online destination for all of their needs," says Leslie Lane, global vice president and general manager for Nike Running. "From finding the right gear, the latest event details, tracking progress, and connecting to friends through Nike+, we're helping runners hit a new stride."[9]

The site features a menu of social media opportunities as described in Nike press releases. They include the following:

- Personalization: The new navigational system includes a customizable homepage for members, providing at-a-glance views of individual training, progress in goals and challenges, and Nike+Mini. Now runners can personalize every run to illustrate their mood, weather, terrain, route, and more.
- Find Your Friends: Runners can search for like-minded and similarly skilled runners, accept new friend requests, and initiate challenges in conjunction with their favorite social media platforms. And because no good run should go unpublished, runners can broadcast their own successes beyond Nike+ with automatic updates to Facebook status, Twitter feeds, and much more.
- Upgraded Challenges: Once runners tap into their own personal running network, Nike+ will recommend challenges from the gallery to inspire a little healthy competition with other runners who have similar running styles or profiles.
- New Shoe Finder: This feature asks runners to answer a few simple questions to receive a customized shoe recommendation based on the latest shoe technology.
- Improved Goals and Challenges: Along with the helpful news, training tips, and event specifics, the site features professional coaching programs from some of Nike's top running coaches and athletes. Runners can choose from a preset coaching program or customize their own routine and goals.

A Nike+ iPhone mobile site, which would give users access to the Nike+data from anywhere, was being discussed at the time I wrote this book.

The Nike+ site was launched in 2006 and within three years, members had logged more than 100 million miles. DeBiase observes,

> When runners upload their data to the site, it becomes a virtual gathering place. In August 2009 alone, 800,000 runners logged onto the site and signed up to run simultaneously in a Nike-sponsored 10K race in 25 cities around the world. Buoyed by the success of this site, Nike is now testing a social networking site aimed at the basketball-playing community as a means to promote its basketball shoes.
>
> Nike may have established a blueprint for other consumer products to emulate as it has adopted a very different strategy. Many companies have tried to build virtual communities centered around their brands. But for Nike, it was never about converting some percentage of users to buy Nike shoes. It was about creating a social network for dedicated runners.

Even before Facebook and Twitter became the hottest buzzwords, Nike had adopted an integrated approach to marketing that utilized the Internet. The company's "Secret Tournament" campaign in 2002 was described by Nike as a "truly integrated, global marketing effort" that departed from the traditional "big athlete, big ad, big product" formula. Instead, a multifaceted consumer experience was utilized in celebration of the FIFA (Federation Internationale de Football Association) World Cup.

The "Secret Tournament" initiative merged advertising and public relations with the Internet and retail events to create enthusiasm for Nike's soccer products and athletes. This modern integrated approach to reaching customers has become the foundation of the company's marketing and communications efforts in the 21st Century.

The "Secret Tournament" campaign, which was estimated to cost $100 million, revolved around a fictional tournament with eight teams of three people, who just happened to be 24 top soccer players. The campaign was highlighted by a Web site where individuals could go to follow the tournament results and play interactive games.

Mark Parker, president and CEO of NIKE, Inc., described the football marketing initiative as "the most comprehensive and successful global campaign ever executed by Nike."

Parker was listed in late 2009 as number 20 on the *Advertising Age* annual roundup of "Power Players." A press release published by *Advertising Age* states: "Nike is the world's dominant footwear and apparel provider, and perhaps its most accomplished digital marketer, as well. That's a direct reflection on Mr. Parker, who has emphasized marketing, and digital marketing in particular, since replacing Bill Perez as CEO in early 2006."

The *Advertising Age* article points to Nike's use of viral videos as a strategy for promoting content and attracting millions of views. It specifically mentions the company's "Next Level" soccer films and the groundbreaking NikePlus, which we have already discussed.

Fast Company magazine, which tracks the best examples of innovation across industry sectors, calls Nike's use of social networking the company's "latest masterstroke."[10]

Nike's ability to continually change its marketing strategy to coincide with the most recent technology used by consumers is widely recognized. In fact, I was recently reading a book called *Get Content Get Customers* and I quickly noticed the first chapter started with a word that caught my attention—Nike. Authors Joe Pulizzi and Newt Barrett use Nike as an example that shows the shift to content marketing. Pulizzi is founder and chief content officer for Junta42, a leading online resource for content marketing; and Barrett is president of Content Marketing Strategies, a firm that assists companies in marketing their products and services by using relevant content.

The first paragraph of their book is relevant to the evolution of Nike's advertising campaigns. Pulizzi and Barrett begin by saying,

> Nike and other huge companies such as Procter & Gamble, Johnson & Johnson, and General Motors are all moving away from basic advertising and sponsorship strategies that helped make their brands as well known as they are today. . . . We are seeing nothing less than a marketing tsunami that is affecting businesses of every size, regardless of what they're selling. Prospects are simply not responding to the kinds of marketing that have worked for decades. So marketing organizations are asking, What now?

Apparently, Nike officials have not encountered any difficulties in answering that particular question. The company's growing use of interactive Web sites is just one example of smart marketing that is working. Pulizzi and Barrett describe content marketing as "the art of understanding exactly what your customers need to know and delivering it to them in a relevant and compelling way." They believe this new method of connecting with customers must extend beyond offering product information and into the realm of best practices, case studies, thought leadership, success stories, and much more. Nike leaders agree.

"We want to find a way to enhance the experience and services, rather than look for a way to interrupt people from getting to where they want to go," says Stefan Olander, global director for brand connections at Nike. "How can we provide a service where the customer says, 'Wow, you really made this easier for me?'"[11]

It all goes back to what Skoloda recommends about the need for companies to connect with customers in a meaningful manner. Nike is doing it effectively and, of course, has the budget to splurge. We will discuss how much money Nike earns each year from the sale of its products in a later chapter. The numbers are large and financial analysts predict they will continue to grow. Once you see how much money the company earns, the amount it spends on advertising is small by comparison. And Knight probably does not hate advertising as much now as he reportedly did when Wieden+Kennedy was first hired to create campaigns for Nike.

CHINESE CULTURE TAKES OFFENSE TO COMMERCIAL

The company hit a snag with its marketing machine in 2004 when China banned a Nike commercial that showed Cleveland Cavaliers' LeBron James fighting a cartoon kung fu master, beating two dragons, and battling women who were dressed in Chinese clothes. The commercial, referred to as "Chamber of Fear," aired on Chinese stations briefly before being pulled.

The State Administration for Radio, Film and Television in China issued a statement at the time saying, "The advertisement violates regulations that mandate all advertisements in China should uphold national dignity and interest, and respect the motherland's culture. It also goes against rules that require ads not to contain content that blasphemes national practices and cultures. The ad has received an indignant response from Chinese viewers."[12]

James, who reportedly signed a $90-million endorsement contract with Nike after coming straight out of high school, responded that the ads were never intended to hurt anybody or to insult any culture. James is a fan of martial arts icon and actor Bruce Lee, and the ads were based on his films.

As the NBA's Most Valuable Player, James is trying to set an example for youths to follow. He kicked off a world tour by visiting London in September 2009 not only to promote the Air Max LeBron VII, but also to talk about the movie, *More Than a Game*. The documentary tells the story of James' triumphant journey to the big time. He offers these thoughts about his trip and the movie:

> Visiting London to launch the Air Max LeBron VII and talk about a movie that follows me and my friends' lives growing up together is something you never think could happen to you. Hopefully, *More Than a Game* will enable kids all around the

world to learn that they can achieve their dreams and goals through hard work and perseverance, not just in basketball but in whatever they decide to do in life. We can all give back and make a difference in many different ways, which I hope to convey and lead by example.[13]

RECOVERING FROM THE KUNG FU MISTAKE

The debacle with the kung fu commercials is proof that nobody gets it right all of the time, not even Nike. The difference is that when Nike commits a faux pas, the company has the cash and creativity to recover and to follow one mistake with another success.

In reference to the amount of money Nike shells out each year to promote its products, *Advertising Age* has released a list of the 100 leading national advertisers. Nike is right in the middle at number 50, while Procter & Gamble continues to dump a whopping $4.8 billion into annual advertising to remain perched at the top of the list. The same article that discusses Mark Parker being a Power Player, continues:

Nike's U.S. ad budget is $790 million, and it has leveraged that spend to a position of almost unfathomable dominance in this market, which has continued throughout a recession that's been tough on pricy shoes. In September (2009), for instance, Nike's three top brands—Nike, Jordan and Converse—grew 11 percent, while major competitors such as Adidas, Reebok and New Balance posted double-digit declines.

The Jordan Brand, which debuted in 1997, has become so powerful that it seems almost unnecessary to keep calling it a division of Nike, even though that's precisely what it is. A November 16, 2009, article by Jeremy Mullman in *Advertising Age* states the Jordan Brand is now bigger than the combined efforts of Nike's merged rivals, Adidas and Reebok, despite a unique distribution strategy that purposely makes it difficult to find the shoes.

"Jordan has established itself as the premiere designer brand in athletic footwear," says long-time footwear analyst Matt Powell, who estimates the shoes are only available in about 10 percent of the locations that carry Nike products. "This is the top-end, conspicuous-consumption brand."[14]

Chapter Four

Become Legendary

Since Michael Jordan played a pivotal role in Nike's comeback in the mid-1980s, I thought it was important to devote a chapter to this division of the company and to the man himself. Jordan, holder of two Olympic gold medals for his participation on Team USA in 1984 and 1992, was inducted into the Naismith Memorial Hall of Fame in September 2009. His career includes being named the NBA's Most Valuable Player in 1988, 1991, 1992, 1996, and 1997.

"The game of basketball has been everything to me," he said in his acceptance speech at the induction ceremony. He thanked not only friends and family members, but surprisingly he also listed the people who never showed any confidence in his ability, most notably the coach who cut him from the high school basketball team.

"I wanted to make sure you understood. You made a mistake, dude," he told those in attendance as if speaking directly to the high school coach.[1]

If the coach is still alive today, I'm sure he realized his error shortly after cutting Jordan from the team. During Jordan's freshman year at the University of North Carolina, he played for a National Collegiate Athletic Association (NCAA) championship team and scored the winning shot in the title game. He earned the title of College Player of the Year from *The Sporting News* in 1983 and 1984. Following his junior year, he was selected in the 1984 draft by the Chicago Bulls. By this time, that high school coach must have been questioning his own coaching decisions.

Jordan's Hall of Fame speech included insight into the difficulty he encountered in achieving acceptance from others in the profession. He obviously never had any difficulty in playing the sport since he is now regarded as possibly the greatest basketball player of all time, playing for both the Chicago Bulls and later for the Washington Wizards. He recalled how members of the media compared him to other players during his early career, but specified that he would never win like Larry Bird or Magic Johnson. He recalls,

Former Chicago Bulls and Washington Wizards guard Michael Jordan gets emotional during his induction into the Naismith Basketball Hall of Fame in September 2009. (AP Photo/ Stephan Savoia)

I had to listen to all that and it put so much wood on the fire that it kept me each and every day trying to get better as a basketball player. I wanted to prove to you, Magic, Larry, George Gervin, everybody that I deserved to be there just as much as anybody else, and I hope over the period of my career I've done that without a doubt.[2]

He more than proved the naysayers wrong and went on to garner five Most Valuable Player awards and six NBA championships to add to his biographical profile. Nike officials recognized his talent when he was just starting to gain fame and fortune, quickly getting him to sign on the dotted line to endorse the first AIR JORDAN shoe in 1985. Unveiling a new version of the AIR JORDAN has been an annual event every year since then.

The Nike Web site describes the history of the AIR JORDAN division:

Each unveiling has been met with ever-increasing anticipation from the media, the industry, and the buying public. AIR

JORDANs perennially dominate the market in sales and demand, establishing with each year's model higher benchmark standards in design, innovation, and performance for the entire athletic footwear industry. At the heart of the franchise is the perfect synergy between athlete and technology—Michael Jordan, the greatest player in the history of basketball, and the shoes he's worn throughout his illustrious career that epitomize his relentless dedication to performance, innovation, and achievement.

With each shoe taking on its own identity, the famous Nike Swoosh symbol eventually was removed and replaced by a "jump-man" logo, depicting a man with a basketball leaping into the air. Any shoe with this logo is specific to the Jordan Brand. The shoes are more difficult to find than other Nike products and tend to be a bit more expensive. Footwear analysts say the shoes are priced comparably to other teenage status symbols, such as iPods.

AIR JORDAN 2010 went on sale at a suggested retail price of $170 in February. Dwyane (odd spelling, but pronounced like Dwayne) Wade, who plays for the Miami Heat, was the first professional athlete to debut this innovative shoe. He is now on the roster of athletes who comprise what is referred to as Team Jordan, which is just another way of naming the players who endorse the Jordan Brand products.

"As a kid, I grew up on the south side of Chicago idolizing Michael Jordan and have worked hard to achieve the same success that he's had on the court," remembers Wade. "I have enormous respect for this brand and all that it stands for. I'm humbled to be part of the Team Jordan family and I'm looking forward to a great future."[3]

Wade, often referred to by sportscasters as "Flash" or "D-Wade," has earned many honors. He is a gold medal winner, just like Jordan, for his part on the U.S. team in the 2008 Summer Olympics. In addition, he is a five-time All Star who was named Most Valuable Player in 2006, the same year he helped the Heat win the world championship.

"In his short time in the league, Dwyane has transformed himself into one of the game's best and is the embodiment of leadership both on and off the court, a signature trait of our athletes," says Jordan. "As the Jordan franchise approaches its silver anniversary, Dwyane will become a pinnacle member of the Jordan roster poised to help lead the brand for years to come."[4]

The AIR JORDAN 2010 represents a collaboration between the shoe's namesake; Tinker Hatfield, vice president of special projects/design for Nike; and Mark Smith, creative director for the Jordan Brand. The result was the development of the brand's first see-through performance basketball shoe designed with a transparent thermoplastic urethane window on the side.

Dwyane Wade, guard for the Miami Heat, gets ready to pass the ball in an NBA game against the Denver Nuggets in December 2009. (AP Photo/David Zalubowski)

Hatfield says the AIR JORDAN 2010 pays homage to Jordan's ability to know his opponents' next move while only giving hints of his ability, and allowing the players to only see what he wanted them to see on the court. "His keen instinct for anticipating his challengers' next move and disguising his own techniques are just a few of the attributes that led to him being named the greatest player ever to play the game."[5]

The shoe features a layered-toe construction with an independent forefoot support cover, which enables the AIR JORDAN 2010 to imitate the foot's flexibility and movement without being restricted. The innovative design represents a unique concept in performance footwear to help players become more agile.

The AIR JORDAN 2009 represented the first time the shoe was not given a number from one to 23. As I mentioned previously, the first shoe was called AIR JORDAN I, followed by AIR JORDAN II all the way up to AIR JORDAN XX3 in 2008. The shoe released in 2009 marked the start of a new period and the retirement of the labels AIR JORDAN I through XX3 to preserve the uniqueness of Jordan's legacy.

"Throughout the first 23 years of the AIR JORDAN franchise, we challenged ourselves and the industry by producing athletic footwear beyond the limits of what was possible," said Jordan when the shoe was unveiled. "The AIR JORDAN 2009 ushers in a new chapter for the brand. It is the embodiment of what we can do and sets the course for the next 23 years for the franchise."[6]

Jordan worked with Jason Mayden, the senior footwear designer for the brand, to create the 2009 version. A new concept called Articulated Propulsion Technology, which enables athletes to quickly propel forward, was used in this particular futuristic-looking shoe. Designers say this is the first AIR JORDAN that incorporates satin pleats and leather that can actually be polished, giving it even more of a high-end appeal.

Shortly after the release of AIR JORDAN 2009, the brand announced the release of a signature shoe for Chris Paul of the New Orleans Hornets. The shoe is called the Jordan CP3.11 because it marks the second shoe created with Paul's lightning fast speed in mind. Designers say they took their cue from futsal, an international game of indoor soccer where fast foot patterns and agile movements are essential.

"It's an amazing honor to have my very own signature shoe with the Jordan Brand and to celebrate its launch right here in New Orleans," says Paul. "There are several elements that have been influenced by my childhood in Winston-Salem and my life now in the Big Easy. New Orleans has become and will always be a big part of my life."[7]

Mayden says the way Paul plays basketball was a big factor when creating the shoe. He wanted the final product to look good and also meet Paul's high-performance needs. He describes Paul's quickness as "his most deadly weapon."

"When he has the ball in his hands, he is like a high-performance motorcycle among a group of slow moving cars," says Mayden. "We designed the CP3.11 with that in mind and created a shoe that is versatile enough to withstand the rapid changes of pace, the break-neck speed, and the pinpoint agility of Chris Paul's style of basketball."[8]

The personalized design of the shoe seemed a bit odd to me at first. However, once I remembered how much Nike caters to these athletes, it was not so surprising that the shoe basically is a three-dimensional biography of Paul. The design honors the faith, family, and friends who have played a role in the basketball player's success.

The number 61 was included on the shoe in memory of Paul's grandfather and the initials CJ are included in honor of his brother. Designers went so far as to include the name of the late Skip Prosser, who was a coach at Wake Forest. Paul's birthday is also noted on the heel and his parents' names are included on the outsole.

It is difficult to find fault with the Jordan Brand, despite some of the company's efforts to personalize the shoes for the celebrities. Overall, the brand has lived up to the caliber of its namesake not just with the quality of its flagship shoes, but also with the other aspects of the division. For example, it also includes the Jordan Sports Performance apparel collections; the Jordan Lifestyle streetwear collection; and Jordan Women, an apparel collection that targets the urban chic female.

Although apparel is available, the shoes are the bread-and-butter products that have sustained the brand for a quarter of a century. I have to reflect again on the AIR JORDAN XX3 because I was pleased the company used this product to revere the accomplishments of Jordan.

Before brand officials decided to stop using the traditional Roman numeral system to distinguish each year's version of the shoe, AIR JORDAN XX3 made a spectacular entrance onto the athletic footwear stage. The shoe was intended to celebrate the heritage of the brand that was sparked by a basketball legend. Jordan issued these heart-felt words when the shoe was unveiled:

> The AIR JORDAN XX3 is deeply meaningful to me as a celebration of both my life and career. The number 23 is obviously of great significance to me and the release of the XX3 is a pinnacle moment in the brand's history. I'm honored and humbled by the AIR JORDAN franchise's loyal following after all these years. The release of this shoe is exciting and a dream come true for me.[9]

The 23rd shoe in the series represents the first to incorporate the Nike Considered Design ethos, which means the development focuses on using environmentally friendly materials, whenever possible. The design minimizes waste and the use of solvent-based cements. In addition, the outsoles are made of an environmentally friendly rubber and include a recycling component by using materials from footwear manufacturing waste.

The AIR JORDAN XX3 sports many unique design features with an imprint of Jordan's fingerprint traction pattern on the outsole, his signature on the toe cap, and his thumbprint on the back of the tongue lining. The shoes have a dual-density sock liner, an internal foam that conforms to the shape of the foot for a custom fit, a compression-molded phylon midsole, a nu-foam collar/tongue lining, quilted sock liner that provides arch support, reinforced quarter panels, a breathable tongue that allows air to escape while keeping the foot cool, a carbon fiber/acrylic weave shank plate for support, high-performance chassis for stability, and advanced cushioning. All of these amenities are included in a shoe that weighs only 15 ounces. Talk about cramming as much technology as possible into one lightweight product. Mission accomplished.

TEAM JORDAN REACHES INTO THE COMMUNITY

The athletes who are members of Team Jordan must possess the same qualities that Jordan believes were important in his career, including dedication, excellence, innovation, and achievement. A portion of the proceeds netted by the brand are donated to Jordan Fundamentals, an educational grants program established in 1999 for teachers. Information about the program is available at www.jordanfundamentals.com.

"The Fundamentals Grant Program was born out of my firm belief that education is the key to opportunity and to building commitment among students to the core values which foster personal excellence and achievement," notes Jordan. "These grants are intended to support teachers and provide access to additional resources that help students succeed."[10]

According to information provided on the Jordan Brand Web site, $1 million is awarded annually to teachers throughout the United States who motivate and inspire students to strive for excellence. The program honors outstanding teachers and instructional creativity in public secondary schools serving economically disadvantaged students. The grants are used to provide resources to enhance instructional creativity and to further curriculum development.

"The grants give teachers the support to try new and innovative ideas in the classroom," explains Jennifer Stimpson, a 2009–2010 recipient who teaches at the Yvonne A. Ewell Townview Magnet Center in Dallas. "These grants inspire educators to motivate students to pursue academic excellence by providing access to important resources that previously may not have been available."[11]

During the past decade, more than $10 million has been provided in grants to teachers at schools where at least 50 percent of the student population is eligible for free or reduced lunch programs.

As an extension of the Jordan Fundamentals Grant Program, Dwyane Wade hosted a pep rally at Miami Norland Senior High School in November. He was a surprise guest, who received an enthusiastic reception. The "Layups for Learning" event, hosted by the Jordan Brand, gave five students a chance to score a layup and earn grant money for their school. Wade told the students about his childhood and his professional basketball experience, as well as the importance of education and being a volunteer for worthwhile causes.

"It was great to be able to join the Jordan Brand in giving back to Miami Norland Senior High School," says Wade. "I feel so blessed to be where I am, so it's important to me that I try to encourage as many youths as I can about the importance of believing in themselves and giving back to their communities. It's amazing to think what the next generation can accomplish."[12]

Serving as emcee at the school pep rally was Jordan Brand Vice President Howard White, who spoke to the students about working hard to reach their dreams. He said the brand was proud to make a donation to the school as an extension of the Jordan Fundamentals program, an effort that was born out of Jordan's belief that education is key to every opportunity. "We are lucky to have an elite Team Jordan athlete like Dwyane assist us in becoming more involved in the Miami community."[13]

The grant amount was not disclosed in Nike press materials.

The athletes who have joined Team Jordan are proud to be associated with a brand that espouses such high ideals regarding community outreach and education.

"Being a part of Team Jordan is something special," adds Derek Jeter of the New York Yankees. "It means we share the values and commitment of the Jordan Brand and will help take it into the future."[14]

In the true spirit of Michael Jordan, the brand presented a $100,000 check to the Make-A-Wish Foundation in February 2009. The money was used to grant two teenagers their wishes, which included attending an All-Star basketball game and a weekend of All-Star activities, as well as meeting Jordan and Paul. A third wish was granted in the following weeks to a recipient who requested a shopping spree in New York City and a laptop computer signed by his favorite athletes.

Jordan, who has granted more than 175 wishes during the past two decades, was appropriately named chief wish ambassador and national spokesman for the Foundation a month earlier. He is now devoting time to helping the organization obtain more grant money nationwide.

"These kids are incredibly brave and their stories are beyond inspiring," said Jordan in a press release dated February 12, 2009. "On behalf of the Jordan Brand, our Team Jordan athletes, and myself, we'd like to thank the Make-A-Wish Foundation for providing us with the opportunity to make wishes come true for these amazing children and their supportive families."

ATTRACTING STAR ENTERTAINMENT

The brand is active in the high school level by sponsoring the Jordan Brand Classic, which brings together the country's top seniors to play each April at Madison Square Garden. Many of the previous event participants, including Chris Paul, have gone on to become NCAA superstars. The 2009 Classic featured the five highest ranked players in the ESPNU's Top 100—names you may see in the future as marvels in the NCAA. They are Xavier Henry, Derrick Favors, DeMarcus Cousins, John Henson, and Renardo Sidney.

The 2009 Classic was highlighted with a half-time performance by hip-hop artist and producer Akon, who is known for his singles "Locked Up" and "Smack That." Brand officials believe the appearance of the SRC Universal Motown recording artist elevated the annual event to a new level.

"An artist of Akon's caliber brings with him an authentic sound and unique style, and turns an event into an experience, taking the Jordan Brand Classic to a whole new level," says Reggie Saunders, director of entertainment marketing for Jordan Brand.[15]

The Jordan Brand has relied heavily on the "Become Legendary" campaign that integrates digital components on www.Jumpman23.com with in-store marketing, as well as consumer, community, and celebrity events. The company launched its latest edition of the campaign in October 2009 with the intention of showing youths the importance of teamwork.

The advertisements embody what the brand represents and epitomize Jordan's legacy of team leadership. The campaign includes a national television marketing effort starring Team Jordan athletes Wade, Paul, Jeter, and Carmelo Anthony of the Denver Nuggets. The commercial is highlighted by numerous visual and audio cuts depicting the athletes' team-building efforts and ultimate success.

ALL-STAR JORDAN BRAND ROSTER

In addition to Wade, Paul, Jeter, and Anthony, other members of Team Jordan, who are selected by Jordan himself, include the following:

- Ray Allen, Guard, Boston Celtics
- Derek Anderson, Guard/Forward, Charlotte Bobcats
- Mike Bibby, Point Guard, Sacramento Kings
- Dre Bly, Cornerback, Denver Broncos
- Michael Finley, Guard/Forward, San Antonio Spurs
- Ahman Green, Running Back, Houston Texans
- Richard Hamilton, Guard/Forward, Detroit Pistons
- Marvin Harrison, Wide Receiver, Indianapolis Colts
- Josh Howard, Guard/Forward, Dallas Mavericks
- Juwan Howard, Forward, Minnesota Timberwolves
- Jared Jefferies, Forward, New York Knicks
- Andruw Jones, Center Fielder, Atlanta Braves
- Eddie Jones, Guard/Forward, Dallas Mavericks
- Freddie Jones, Guard, New York Knicks
- Joe Johnson, Guard/Forward, Atlanta Hawks

- Terrell Owens, Wide Receiver, Dallas Cowboys
- Mickael Pietrus, Guard/Forward, Golden State Warriors
- Quentin Richardson, Guard/Forward, New York Knicks
- Warren Sapp, Defensive Lineman, Oakland Raiders
- Bobby Simmons, Forward, Milwaukee Bucks
- Jason Taylor, Defensive End, Miami Dolphins
- Gerald Wallace, Forward, Charlotte Bobcats

One more name should be, or perhaps one day will be, included on the list of Team Jordan athletes. It's none other than Marcus Jordan, who is already exhibiting the same values as his famous father, Michael. As a student and basketball guard at the University of Central Florida, the young Jordan caused a stir in late 2009 when he refused to wear Adidas shoes. He instead opted to wear a pair of white AIR JORDANs, saying the shoes have a special meaning for his family. He did, however, agree to wear all other Adidas apparel.

University of Central Florida basketball player Marcus Jordan is introduced along with his teammates during half-time at an NCAA game against the University of Miami in October 2009. (AP Photo/Phelan M. Ebenhack)

The university was in the last year of a $3-million deal with Adidas that mandated athletes and coaches wear the company's apparel and use its equipment. As a result of Jordan's refusal to wear the shoes, Adidas decided not to continue its relationship with the university.

"The University of Central Florida has chosen not to deliver on its contractual commitment to Adidas," Andrea Corso, Adidas spokeswoman told the *Associated Press*. "As a result, we have chosen not to continue our relationship with them moving forward."[16]

The university later released a statement responding to the action taken by Adidas. "We are disappointed to learn that Adidas has chosen to discontinue its relationship with UCF Athletics," said Joe Hornstein, spokesman for the university. "Once we receive official notice, we will be able to further respond."[17]

From a legal standpoint, I understand why Adidas had to respond to what it probably viewed as a breach of contract. However, Marcus was merely taking the necessary action to remain true to his beliefs even in the face of controversy and potential repercussion. Although neither his dad nor Nike have responded publicly, I'm sure they are both proud of Marcus. It is always easier to do what other people expect, or want, us to do. However, it takes real courage to defend our principles as Marcus did. His steadfast devotion to his father and the Jordan Brand reminds me of the relentless commitment that was required in order for Knight and Bowerman to build Nike from scratch.

The incident involving Marcus is merely a reflection of a son's pride for his father. However, if Nike is trying to have an overwhelming influence on college sports, the company scored a touchdown in 2009 with its presence at the Ohio State University versus the University of Michigan game. The company knows how to wield its influence in a variety of venues, including college sports.

Chapter Five

Setting Precedents in College Sports

"The tail is now wagging the dog."

That's how Kenneth Halloy describes Nike's penetration into the realm of college sports. Halloy is president of Halloy Boy Sports Marketing, Inc., a Columbus, Ohio, company that publishes football magazines, produces special sports events, and provides consulting services. He has also co-hosted *This Week in Football* on a radio station in Columbus, which is home of the Ohio State Buckeyes.

Ohio State University (OSU) has always maintained a strong following and been known as the football team to beat. Under the leadership of Head Football Coach Jim Tressel, Ohio State captured its fifth consecutive Big Ten Conference Championship on November 21, 2009. The 21–10 victory over the University of Michigan represented the 106th matchup between the schools, but this particular game had a special meaning for Ohio State as a result of Nike's involvement.

Ohio State veered from tradition during this major rivalry to sport one-time tribute uniforms to commemorate the 55th anniversary of the university's 1954 undefeated national championship team. The uniforms, which were part of Nike's Pro Combat line, featured white helmets with a red stripe down the middle and black numbers on the side, white jerseys with scarlet numbers and a splash of gray on the shoulders, along with gray pants that had a double scarlet stripe down the side. What the players were wearing provided plenty of conversation fodder for sports analysts and staunch Ohio State fans like Halloy. He points out,

> The Ohio State University boasts the nation's largest athletics program with more than 30 varsity sports. For Ohio State to break tradition and wear a throwback uniform in *the game* against its arch rival is saying a mouthful. Now, it's not necessarily a bad thing to see tradition broken. In fact, many OSU traditionalists, including yours truly, who were initially appalled by the throwback jersey agreement, discovered afterward that the

Ohio State University Head Football Coach Jim Tressel spends time with his players before the team defeated the University of Michigan in the big matchup in November 2009. The OSU players wore Nike-designed uniforms to honor the 1954 championship team. (AP Photo/Paul Sancya)

jerseys were actually pretty nice looking. And lo and behold, the world didn't come to an end after all.

Nike collaborated with Ohio State players and athletic department personnel to design the uniforms, which Coach Tressel believes added another dimension to the championship game.

"It's an awesome responsibility to play in the Ohio State–Michigan game and it adds a little bit more when all of a sudden you're wearing what the people did that were extraordinary in another given year," says Tressel. "It seems to be the kind of thing that's done all over the place now. I'm a little old school, but even I'm trying to mature a little bit and embrace things like that."[1]

The Nike Pro Combat gear is 37 percent lighter than regular uniforms and features a four-way stretch twill designed to resist sweat and water, making it 46 percent lighter when wet. Even if the Pro Combat uniform was drenched by rain, it would still be lighter than a completely dry version of Ohio State's current design. The Nike uniform has a padded base layer, made of dual-density foam cells to absorb, deflect, and disperse the impact of tough hits and injuries. A foam grid intersects the cells to enhance impact absorption and improve flexibility. A plastic shield covers the thigh padding for added protection.[2]

"Nike offered us a chance to try a new uniform product featuring cutting-edge fabrics and technology," notes Gene Smith, director of athletics at Ohio State.[3]

The Ohio State players were anxious to wear the uniforms, which actually appeared to be quite modern rather than out of style.

"It is great representing the 1954 team," says OSU senior defensive lineman Doug Worthington. "We're interested in wearing them because it represents a great team that deserves the recognition. This might go on from year to year now—changing throwbacks and wearing different jerseys for the Michigan game."[4]

Although the players might think wearing different uniforms for the Michigan rivalry each year is a good idea, OSU has not indicated whether this will become a trend. However, Halloy believes that Nike has set a far-reaching precedent by convincing Ohio State to wear the Pro Combat uniforms. He says,

> A precedent was set for the rest of the college sports world. If the nation's largest athletics department needs Nike and will follow its directives, it only goes to reason that the rest of the nation's athletics programs will also follow. Nike operates with the luxury of knowing that schools are constantly battling a financial crunch when it comes to operating their athletic programs, not to mention the continually skyrocketing salaries of football and basketball coaches. For example, it was recently announced that University of Texas Football Coach Mack Brown is getting a raise with his annual salary jumping from $3 million to $5 million.

Halloy points out that Nike's influence on college sports should be closely monitored because there is a potential "danger" of where the company's power could lead.

"Nike may ultimately impact the national championship football game and that's not necessarily a bad thing. At the end of the day, Nike has money. Money is power. Power can be good or evil," he says. "Thus far, Nike's influence (on college sports) has been positive."

Nike provided Pro Combat basketball uniforms for five college teams to wear in their NCAA conference tournaments and championship games in 2009. Teams selected to wear the apparel and customized footwear were Duke University, Gonzaga University, the University of Memphis, Michigan State University, and the University of Oregon.[5]

"College basketball is a tremendously quick and physical game, and Nike is committed to giving student athletes the best gear for battle," says Todd Van Horne, creative director for Nike's Sport Apparel and Innovation. "Nike Pro Combat reflects the evolution of the game and provides our college teams with quality base layer apparel they need for their tournament runs."[6]

The hips and thighs are protected with the Pro Combat Deflex shorts and the elbows are covered with unsurpassed padding. The shorts and the elbow sleeves reflected each team's colors. The light-weight jerseys, made of an engineered mesh to promote cooling, were designed to depict each university's special identity. The Duke jersey, for example, was inspired by the campus chapel and the university's overall heritage.[7]

Duke University Basketball Coach Mike Krzyzewski, one of the preeminent college coaches in the country, believes it was a huge honor to be selected to wear the Nike apparel. He says it made the players even more proud than they typically are when playing in the conference tournaments. I was extremely pleased that such a high-caliber coach agreed to provide comments for my book. Not only is Krzyzewski well-known for coaching the Duke players, but he also coached the 2008 U.S. Men's Olympic Basketball Team, which brought home a gold medal.

When asked whether he thought the Pro Combat system made a difference in the comfort and performance of the players, he replied that it has helped.

"A player might be more aggressive and open to physical contact having the support and protection that this apparel provides. It helps

Duke University Basketball Coach Mike Krzyzewski reacts to a play during a recent game. (Courtesy of the Duke University Sports Information Department)

in the prevention of injury when the anticipation of injury is reduced," says Krzyzewski. "We believe that Nike provides Duke with the best equipment. That is why we have remained partners for such a long period of time."

During his 30-year career at Duke University, Krzyzewski has gained tremendous insight into how college players think and react to various situations. He says the young players clearly recognize Nike's position of having the most powerful brand in sports. However, he does not believe they fully understand the overall impact that Nike has made on athletics, even though many of the sports stars are fairly young when the company initially sponsors them. Consider, for example, Adrian Peterson, who was born in 1985 and left college after two years to begin his career with the Minnesota Vikings. LeBron James, formerly of the Cleveland Cavaliers was under contract with Nike shortly after graduating from high school.

Krzyzewski says certain words come to mind when he thinks about what Nike means to college athletics and professional sports.

"Excellence. Integrity. The company understands athletes because of Phil Knight's influence," he adds. "Nike has always been about enhancing the performance of the people playing that sport. Hopefully, they'll never lose that since that has always been the core of what they do for sports."

The Pro Combat system of dress used for the college athletes also included the Nike Hyperdunk shoe made with the high-tech Flywire support system. Nike began testing the Pro Combat base layer system during the 2008 Summer Olympics in Beijing, China, when members of the U.S. Men's Basketball Team, including Kobe Bryant, LeBron James, and Carmelo Anthony, wore the special padding. Incidentally, the American players brought home a gold medal and earned the name "Redeem Team" for making a comeback after the U.S. men's basketball team was defeated by Argentina in the 2004 Olympics in Greece.[8]

The American team had a tremendously positive force on its side in 2008. It was not the Nike apparel, but the experience and expertise of Coach Krzyzewski and the management savvy of basketball guru Jerry Colangelo, who served as managing director of the team.

Nike designers say it is important to remember that today's basketball players have evolved along with the faster style of global play. Pro Combat is a breakthrough solution for basketball players engaged in battle in the blocks and on the perimeter. "Its patented energy-absorbing foam redistributes the impact of collisions on the court and provides the ultimate base layer protection," says Van Horne.[9]

Nike stepped up its marketing efforts for the Pro Combat protective system by kicking off a "Prepare for Combat" campaign in September 2009. By this time, Pro Combat was already being used by NFL All-Pro players like Adrian Peterson, Justin Tuck, Brian Urlacher, and

Steven Jackson. The campaign was brilliant with the creation of the "Alter Ego" television commercial starring Peterson. Nike timed the first air date of the commercial to coincide with the NFL's nationally televised season opening game between the Pittsburgh Steelers and the Tennessee Titans.[10]

"The campaign captures the energy, power, and speed of football," says Ken Dice, vice president of North America marketing for Nike. "We put a spotlight on our new Nike Pro Combat protective gear which can help athletes on all levels become a more dominating force on the field."[11]

The "Alter Ego" commercial with Peterson has a science-fiction feel to it and a great finish with the athlete sitting in front of his locker at the end of the game. A three-dimensional overlay of the Pro Combat deflex pattern is shown on Peterson's skin, symbolizing the transformation that athletes can experience if they wear the product.

The amount of hype that surrounds the release of most Nike products may be mind-boggling to many consumers. The athletes peddling these products would be equally effective in their sport no matter what they were wearing. However, Nike intensifies the anticipation surrounding its products by employing unique marketing strategies featuring these athletes.

The company left no stone unturned with the "Prepare for Combat" campaign by kicking things off with a COUNTDOWN2COMBAT digital feature. High school football players could visit the www. nikefootball.com site to take advantage of daily tips, motivational videos, free music downloads, wake-up calls from Nike football athletes, and information on Nike gear. The company partnered with Universal Motown, Island Def Jam, and Interscope Records to produce Game Day Remixes of popular hip-hop songs.[12]

It is hard to talk about any Nike product without drifting into a discussion about the advertising and marketing campaigns that were created to promote it. It's equally difficult to discuss a product without providing specifics about the technology used to create the shoe, apparel, or gear. All aspects of the company are so intertwined that one cannot be completely separated from the others. Therefore, technology and advertising are intermixed with other topics throughout this book.

Another word has occasionally been associated with the company's products, advertising campaigns, and most recently, the athletes who endorse Nike products. That word is *controversy*. I do not like to perpetuate negative information, but if the shoe fits . . .

Chapter Six

When Nike Athletes Stumble

Nike has an arsenal of public relations and marketing people who know how to spin stories in the company's favor, push the products, and take advantage of media opportunities. In certain circumstances, though, the company really does not have to put forth much effort to garner media attention. When one of its sponsored athletes steps out of bounds, the company has to answer the obvious question: Will you continue your relationship with this particular athlete? In most cases, Nike has remained true to the athletes who endorse its products, even when they step out of line with their behavior. In this chapter, we will talk about Tiger Woods, Michael Vick, and Serena Williams.

LET'S TALK TIGER

One of the biggest headlines that captivated people around the world in late 2009 focused not on actual sports events, but on the extramarital activities of golf professional Tiger Woods. It's a sad commentary on society and the state of the news business that so much attention was devoted to covering this story. To a small extent, it might give credence to the fact that society in general values honesty and the sanctity of marriage. However, I think the widespread coverage is more reflective of the public's insatiable desire to hear about other people's dirty laundry.

Plenty of books will be written about the Eldrick "Tiger" Woods story with all of its twists and turns. I am including the information in my book because it is relevant to the story of Nike. In fact, I wanted to include comments from Woods because many people automatically associate him with Nike. I tried to reach Woods for several months through his management company, IMG, which is a sports, entertainment, and media business. I also left numerous messages for Mark Steinberg, who personally represents Woods and serves as the senior corporate vice president and managing director of golf at IMG. My calls were made many months before the scandal broke, but I never received a response. The type of information I had hoped to obtain was simply going to focus on Woods' career and his relationship with Nike. The scandal details would have been just a sidebar. Nike's reaction to the Woods' saga is relevant because of the significant amount of attention placed on the companies that sponsor him.

When Nike signed a deal to give Woods $5 million per year to endorse its products in 1996, the 21-year-old golf prodigy was obviously talented, but still unknown. Critics scoffed at Nike's deal with the young golfer, but Woods proved he was worthy of the sponsorship a year later when he won the Masters by a record 12 strokes. *Forbes* reported in 2000 that Nike had upped its multi-year deal with Woods to $105 million.

Nike officials took a chance on an unknown golfer back in the mid-1990s just days after he turned professional, and the company continued to support him throughout the controversy. The company provided a brief statement via email to the New York-based *MarketWatch* that read: "Nike supports Tiger and his family. Our relationship remains unchanged."[1]

Woods announced on December 11, 2009, that he was walking away from the game of golf to concentrate on his personal matters. He has not missed a Masters Golf Tournament since he first played as an amateur in 1995. He posted the following statement on his Web site:

> After much soul searching, I have decided to take an indefinite break from professional golf. I need to focus my attention on being a better husband, father, and person. I am deeply aware of the disappointment and hurt that my infidelity has caused to so many people, most of all my wife and children. I want to say again to everyone that I am profoundly sorry and that I ask forgiveness. It may not be possible to repair the damage I've done, but I want to do my best to try.

During a conference call in December 2009 announcing its fiscal year 2010 second quarter financial results, Nike CEO and President Mark Parker was asked the obvious question: Can you make any statement about the impact that you see on the business orders and inventories (as a direct result of the Tiger circumstances)? He responded,

> You have to recognize that Nike has about a $650-million golf business, which like the rest of the broader golf market, has really been among the most impacted or probably hardest hit segments of our business, particularly in this economic environment over the past year. That said, I want to quickly add that we feel very good about how we are managing our golf business through this period and our position in the broader golf

Tiger Woods watches an NCAA college football game in California on November 21, 2009, with his wife, Elin Nordegren, and his daughter, Sam. (AP Photo/Marcio Jose Sanchez)

market with confidence in our growth potential going forward. The only thing I'll say right now about Tiger is that we all know he's chosen to step away from the game. We'll respect that and continue to support Tiger and his family as we, of course, look forward to his return.

The youthful innocence and good-boy image personified by Woods made him a dream for companies like Nike and Accenture, both of which provided him with lucrative contracts. That personal image was tarnished, possibly forever, after Woods crashed his vehicle into a tree on November 27, 2009, an incident that sparked a whirlwind of controversy. After the minor accident, numerous women came forward to reveal details about their relationships with the golfer.

The billion-dollar sports star has earned more money from his rewarding endorsement deals than he has from actually playing golf. Companies that have helped to provide a posh lifestyle for him and his wife, Elin, include not only Nike and Accenture, but also Procter & Gamble's brand Gillette, AT&T, Inc., and Swiss watchmaker TAG Heuer.

Woods became a brand ambassador for TAG Heuer in 2002 and the company was still maintaining the relationship as of the beginning of 2010. However, company officials have decided to curtail the use of Woods' image.

"The partnership with Tiger Woods will continue, but we will downscale the use of his image in certain markets for a period of time, depending on his decision about returning to professional golf," says Jean-Christophe Babin, president and CEO of TAG Heuer. "We will continue to actively support the Tiger Woods Foundation."[2]

While most of the companies are continuing to support Woods to some degree, Accenture, Gillette, and AT&T have not been as forgiving. Accenture, a global management consulting, technology services, and outsourcing company, became the first major sponsor to ditch Woods after a six-year relationship that featured a "Go on, be a Tiger" campaign.

An announcement posted on the Accenture Web site states:

For the past six years, Accenture and Tiger Woods have had a very successful sponsorship arrangement and his achievements on the golf course have been a powerful metaphor for business success in Accenture's advertising. However, given the circumstances of the last two weeks, after careful consideration and analysis, the company has determined that he is no longer the right representative for its advertising.

Gillette followed suit, but did so with a more subtle message that stated, "As Tiger takes a break from the public eye, we will support

This 2008 photo shows Tiger Woods with caddie Steve Williams celebrating a win at an Accenture tournament in Arizona. Accenture has since distanced itself from the golfer. (AP Photo/Matt York, File)

his desire for privacy by limiting his role in our marketing programs."[3] That's a very discreet way of saying we agree with Accenture, but we are going to be a bit more ambiguous.

AT&T discontinued its relationship with Woods by boldly and succinctly saying, "We are ending our sponsorship with Tiger Woods and wish him well in the future."[4] The AT&T name and logo had been clearly visible on Woods' golf bag at various competitions.

As for Nike and the other sponsors who are supporting Woods, it appears they recognize this is strictly a personal matter that has no correlation to his ability to play golf. The Professional Golf Association (PGA) Tour supported Woods' decision to step away from his professional career for a few months to address the issues in his personal life. Despite the tabloid sensationalism and criticism, Woods still managed to win the PGA Tour Player of the Year award, which is based on votes from other golfers on the U.S. Tour. The day before winning the honor from his peers, he was named Golfer of the Year by the Golf Writers of America.[5]

"His priorities are where they need to be and we will continue to respect and honor his family's request for privacy," noted PGA Tour Commissioner Tim Finchem. "We look forward to Tiger's return to the PGA Tour when he determines the time is right for him."[6]

Woods has an impressive streak of winning 14 consecutive years on the PGA Tour, just three years behind golf great Jack Nicklaus. Despite his personal setbacks and the loss of endorsements, Woods returned to the links to play in the Augusta National in April. He had hoped to win the Masters, but finished in fourth place.

"If Tiger is going to pass my record, this is a big year for him in that regard," said Nicklaus before Woods announced his return. "If he doesn't play this year, the chore will be a little tougher."[7]

The last time Woods took a hiatus from golf was in 2008 to recover from a knee injury and a double stress fracture in his leg. Nike celebrated the return of their big money-maker at that time by creating "The Good Life" commercial, which began airing in February 2009. The 60-second spot showed Woods, along with other golfers Stewart Cink, Trevor Immelman, Anthony Kim, Justin Leonard, and Carl Petterssen, enjoying their victory celebrations.[8]

"We had a great time shooting the spot together. We had a lot of laughs," said Woods in a Nike press release that was issued to coincide with the commercial.

Nike continued promoting Woods' return in May 2009 by coordinating a "Tiger Web Talkback" event where golf fans were able to visit www.nikegolf.com to hear insights from Woods about playing golf and other related topics. Nike Golf put Woods in touch with consumers around the world via a real-time Internet connection. He was able to talk live to fans in eight U.S. cities.[9]

"I enjoy an opportunity to speak directly to golf fans. It's cool to be able to do it through the cutting-edge technology of the Web," said Woods in a Nike announcement just days before the cyber event.

Mike Francis, U.S. general manager of Nike Golf, called the event a unique experience for consumers "to interlace with our brand, to be inspired by Tiger, and to ignite their passion for golf."[10]

Nike's reaction to Woods' return in 2010 was rather subdued compared to the fanfare of the previous year. The company's effort to make a big splash when Woods returned in 2009 after recovering from his injuries is evidence of their dedication to this athlete. After all, why shouldn't they be forever devoted to the world's top golfer who sports Nike apparel even when he is promoting products for other companies that have sponsored him over the years, including American Express, Buick, Electronic Arts, TAG Heuer, Accenture, and Gillette.

If you review print and television ads where Woods has endorsed non-Nike products, you can clearly see the undeniable Swoosh logo on his shirt, hat, or both. This is a prime example of Nike capitalizing not only on the popularity of its top endorser, but also on the marketing dollars being spent by other companies. The effectiveness of this unusual marketing arrangement that focuses on Woods is readily evident by the mere fact that other sponsors embrace the idea that he wears the Nike apparel in their commercials.

"It's a stretch to say that two brands are being pitched," says Buick spokesman John Wray. "People expect him to be in a Nike hat. It's natural."[11]

Buick originally signed a five-year contract with Woods in 1999 and renewed the deal in 2004 for an undisclosed amount of money. At the time, Wray would not divulge the contract amount, but stressed that Buick sold more than 130,000 Rendezvous sport utility vehicles in 2002 and 2003, when Woods was involved in the marketing. "It has to be in recognition of Tiger," he says.[12]

Woods has publicly expressed the reasoning behind why he is so dedicated to Nike. After listening to his words about how the company played a crucial role in getting his professional career off the ground, it is easy to understand why he perpetually dons the company's apparel. He expressed his gratitude toward Nike during an interview in 2008 that was part of a CNBC special entitled "Swoosh! Inside Nike." A portion of the interview can be seen on www.youtube.com by simply searching for "Tiger Woods: How Nike Helped Launch His Career."

In the interview, Woods states:

> It all started with Nike. They gave me an opportunity to, you know, be head to toe and paid me a contract I really did not deserve because I had not done anything on a professional level and quite frankly, I hadn't played well in any PGA tour event.

Phil Knight had the confidence in me to go ahead and put that kind of money forward which had never been done before. Do I owe them loyalty for that? Yes, because they gave me an opportunity. With the money I received, I was able to go out there and just play, not worry about having to make ends meet. I was very lucky. Not a lot of people have that opportunity, but Nike gave me that and I will always be eternally grateful for that.

In light of the seemingly unbreakable bond between Nike and Woods, it was not surprising the company chose to support him after the allegations surfaced about his extramarital games. Sports analysts, as well as marketing executives, throughout the world were watching to see what sponsors would do when Woods' baby-face façade began to fade. Many marketing aficionados believe Nike is very adept at turning a negative situation into just another opportunity to keep its name in the public eye.

Mark Lando, a former executive and owner of The Athlete's Foot Marketing Associates, Inc., believes the public often puts celebrities on a pedestal and subsequently believes they can do no wrong. When the celebrity makes a mistake, his or her reputation may suffer a black eye. However, Nike often pounces on the opportunity to ride the media blitz.

"How many times did you hear the name Nike on the news regarding Tiger Woods and his alleged transgressions," asks Lando, whose family founded The Athlete's Foot store in Pittsburgh in 1972. "No doubt, Nike will find a way to make it work to their advantage."

Kelley Skoloda, the advertising guru who talked about Nike's marketing campaigns earlier in the book, says the company's strong focus on the professional side of the athletes helps it deal with negative publicity surrounding people like Woods. She says,

Nike's focus on the professional athlete versus the personal side of an athlete helps it dodge the personal tribulations of some of its sponsored athletes. I can't imagine that any company wants to deal with such situations and once an athlete removes himself from the sport, as Tiger Woods did, I think it becomes more difficult for Nike to maintain its focus on just the performance of the professional athlete. Nike's primary focus on the professional performance side versus the personal life of an athlete seems to be in line with its decision to stand by Tiger, while other sponsors, who are more focused on personal discipline or accomplishments, have dropped him.

Skoloda believes Nike commits itself to the best athletes who are at the top of their game and who, therefore, can provide maximum exposure for the company in a way that equates Nike with being the best.

"Nike supports the athletes they sponsor because they are so linked to them from a financial and image perspective," she adds. "In some ways, the antics of certain athletes are actually consistent with Nike's no-holds-barred 'Just Do It' positioning."

Because Skoloda is an expert in marketing initiatives that appeal to women, she was able to add an interesting perspective to the Tiger Woods story. Women are providing an ever-increasing amount of input to companies across all product lines—to such an extent that they are gaining the unofficial titles of "co-brand managers." Skoloda notes,

> I have heard many women comment that they will avoid buying products made by Tiger's sponsors as an expression of their anger for what he did and companies supporting him in spite of his behavior. If female or male Nike customers balk en masse and loudly enough at Nike's support of Tiger, Nike will have some tough decisions to make. Nike should be turning to the input of its key customers and audiences, and turning to what the company's moral compass says to decide whether they drop or keep him. As long as they are consistent with those two guideposts, they will make the best decision for the company and the brand.

By the time this book is published, the controversy over Woods will probably be a thing of the past. However, input from these key marketing professionals is valuable and relevant in explaining why companies make certain choices. The input also may influence how companies, such as Nike, make their decisions in the future regarding the negative actions exhibited by athletes.

The next section features my interview with Dean DeBiase, who also provided valuable insight about Nike's advertising campaigns in chapter three. He expands on important topics touched upon by other industry experts in this chapter.

AN INTERVIEW WITH DEAN DEBIASE

Following is an interview conducted with DeBiase in 2009:

TC: Why do you think Nike is such a staunch supporter of people like Tiger Woods and Serena Williams?

DD: *Nike has built its brand on celebrity endorsements. If it had not put this dominant brand building strategy at the core of its culture, it would not have become the leading brand that it is today. There are several reasons why Nike is willing to an extent to stay with its sponsored athletes while others would or could not.*

First, as an athletic brand, it has a lot more invested in an athlete, such as Tiger Woods, than do brands that are not in the athletic field, such as Accenture. This investment is not just monetary, but emotional. Accenture can move on to other non-sports personalities and sponsorships, but Nike is sports. Period. The ties with the athletes they endorse are much more integral to their brand DNA than it is for Accenture. Secondly, they need to demonstrate to the broader professional athletic community that they are true partners for the sake of their existing and future endorsements. It's a competitive field for endorsements that comes down to not just money, but a connection to the brand and a trusted relationship with the athletic community. Nike must be seen as supporting its athletes in good times and, under certain circumstances, bad.

Finally, and most importantly, they stick with Tiger Woods and Serena Williams because in a way these instances are part of their brand equity of "Just Do It." Granted, the behavior of both athletes was not condoned by Nike and the actions of Tiger Woods are much worse than those of Serena Williams. However, it is part of the whole persona of what "Just Do It" (no pun intended on Tiger Woods' part) is all about. In a very non-conscious way, it actually does substantiate some of the emotion behind it.

TC: Why have other companies dropped Tiger?

DD: *As advertisers, sponsors, the PGA, broadcast and cable networks try to re-measure and adjust the impact of Tiger's absence during the 2010 games, there are others, more opportunistically, who are already planning to profit from his choreographed return to the game and the world of big-brand advertising. While many existing and proposed advertisers, like Accenture, quickly and publicly distance themselves from Tiger, Nike is one of those advertisers who has a smarter, some say more calculated, plan. Though they will say they are standing by him and publicly support him, Nike will pull back on their Tiger investments without publicly distancing themselves from his brand so they can come back stronger when he kicks off his own comeback tour. Other companies simply do not have as much invested in athletics and professional athletes as does Nike and their brand positions or equity are very different from Nike's. Woods' actions are inconsistent with their equity and they can only erode their brand by continued association.*

Also, some brands like Accenture have a track record of running a shorter campaign of one to three years around celebrities and athletes, making it easier to drop the spokesperson and move on to the next hot personality or back-to-basics campaign. Nike cannot just drop their stars because they have too much invested in them and although they always have a cold and calculated option to drop an athlete and move on, that nuclear approach is only taken if there is complete certainty of a non-recovery. Though this Tiger blip is not something they are happy with, a good brand is always prepared for quiet periods with a strategy to go dark for a while and reboot the co-brand with something completely different when the time is right.

TC: Do you think Nike has mastered the art of turning negative situations encountered by its endorsers into opportunities for even more company publicity?

DD: *No, I don't think that is what they are looking to accomplish here. The Nike brand is all about mastering the positive competitiveness in athletes and positive consumer associations to do it (whatever it is) with their brand, their products and in the future, service extensions (also known as ongoing customer relations) with their products. When things turn negative, they are looking for ways to lay low, be supportive, but wait it out. There is nothing positive that can come from aggressively or proactively looking to leverage this because of the nature of the situation.*

TC: Could it hurt Nike in any way by continuing to support Tiger?

DD: *At this point with so much invested, it would hurt Nike more by dropping Tiger than by continuing to support him, providing that they continue to support him in a low-key manner. No one will think poorly of them for standing by someone from whom they have profited when that individual is in trouble. That could change if public opinion degrades to a level that is unsupportable. They have invested significantly in Tiger Woods both monetarily and with the equity of their brand. To drop him now would prevent reaping the full return on their investment in him. It would be premature to do so and not allow them to maximize their ROI on the relationship.*

TC: What marketing impact does Tiger have on Nike, its competitors, and the ecosystem of the game?

DD: *Though Mark Parker said they will "continue to support Tiger and his family as we look forward to his return," this is not good news for Nike or the game for a while. Tiger's participation in tournaments provides dramatic increases in television viewers and massive Nike brand buzz in and around the tour and individual games.*

Tiger's actual presence in the games usually translates into a 50-percent increase in advertising costs compared to games he does not play in. With marketers spending over a half billion dollars a year on television commercials just during the PGA events alone, there is a lot at stake for CBS, NBC, and the PGA. And Nike must alter its approach to take advantage of this historic anomaly.

Without Tiger promoting Nike during these events, the Nike brand will be losing substantial exposure opportunities. However, Nike will have other promotion opportunities and with ad rates lower, they may also want to go on the offensive and buy some ad time to keep their brand top of mind with viewers and closer to the emerging top players on the tour.

With its normal dominant position, Nike typically does not need to buy tons of television ad time on the PGA tour as they are so embedded with Tiger and his coattail, spill-over endorsements. However, with Tiger out and ad rates down, Nike may see competitors, like Under Armour® and others, jump in and buy cheaper ad space in an effort to move ahead of Nike. With the rules of the game suspended for a while, we may see some historic brand wars develop. Nike may begin to shift from their comfortable domination strategy to a more defensive brand position that selectively flanks their opportunistic competitors' marketing moves. Let the new marketing games begin.

TC: How did the Nike/Tiger co-brand break the mold?

DD: *Ultimately, Tiger comprises a small part of Nike's actual advertising. He appears in less than 5 percent of their ads as compared to Accenture, where he appeared in more than 80 percent of their ads. Nike also has other athletes in their stable that help contribute to their brand. There is not as much pressure to drop Tiger as there was for Accenture, which in essence has their brand tied into him as a personality. But for Nike, that is not the entire story. The Nike-Woods co-brand relationship has broken many rules of marketing and has taken athlete branding to a more embedded and systematic level of creativity with very complex contract clauses. With Nike betting more than $100 million on Tiger in a multi-year contract, they knew they had to go beyond standard endorsements and capitalize on his image 24/7 anytime, anywhere he appears. Nike is a huge beneficiary of the 24/7 Tiger because in addition to their promotions, he is pictured in Nike gear in almost all of his other brand endorsements. This brand spill-over is massive for Nike and has allowed them to syndicate their brand across most all of the Tiger ads and appearances—virtually for free. Imagine having your brand appear in all of the TAG, Accenture, and Buick ads without ever having to cut anyone a check or even having to acknowledge or thank them.*

It's no wonder Nike has not had to run a lot of Tiger ads over the years. They don't need to. They have creatively co-marketed and even saturated the market by being embedded with other strong brand campaigns that even target different audiences for them. Many of the other brands liked the iconic Nike association with Buick calling the association natural, inferring consumers expect Tiger to have the Swoosh hat on. With all of the co-marketing momentum hijacked from other Tiger endorsements, it is hard for Nike to measure the impact of Tiger because his image went beyond their own campaigns. However, with all of that momentum building on the way up, the spiral down can be even faster and have a defeating impact on the Nike brand as the other brands pull out or go silent. Though most marketing experts are not worried about the longevity of the Nike brand, the multiplier effect of lost advertising from coattail ad placements will leave a much larger hole for Nike to rebuild from with a new campaign strategy when Tiger returns.

DeBiase's comments reveal a lot about Nike's continued commitment to Tiger. Now, let's consider a few other Nike-sponsored professional athletes who received media attention for all of the wrong reasons.

NIKE SUPPORTS SERENA'S TIRADE

Nike officials looked the other way when tennis champion Serena Williams threw a temper tantrum at the U.S. Open in September 2009. Her profanity-laden outcry included threatening a lineswoman who cited her for a foot fault infraction.

Grand Slam Administrator Bill Babcock announced in late November 2009 that Williams was fined a record $82,500 for her unprofessional behavior and could be suspended from the event, if she commits another major infraction within the next two years.[13]

In a statement released by her Los Angeles-based publicist, Williams stated, "I am thankful that we now have closure to the incident and we can all move forward. I am back in training in preparation for

Tennis champion Serena Williams reacts after winning a point against Spain's Virginia Ruano Pascual at the Roland Garros Stadium in Paris in May 2009. (AP Photo/Christophe Ena)

next season and I continue to be grateful for all of the support from my fans and the tennis community."[14]

She did not thank Nike in that particular statement, but company officials are probably more concerned that Williams reportedly earned more than $6.5 million in prize money in 2009 and will continue to sport the company's apparel. The company released its own statement shortly after Williams' outburst, saying that it backed her.

"Serena has publicly apologized and has stated she let her emotions get the best of her," says Derek Kent, a Nike spokesman. "Nike stands behind Serena and looks forward to her outstanding career continuing."[15]

Adding to the controversy, Williams' U.S. Open outfit included a Nike t-shirt that read "Can't Spell Dynasty without Nasty!"[16] Many viewers felt that she should have been fined based on the sheer audacity and in-your-face brashness of the t-shirt. Whether Nike knew she was going to wear the shirt or whether they endorsed it is open for debate.

MICHAEL VICK FUMBLES

In light of the widespread public sentiment against Vick in 2007 for his involvement in a horrendous dog-fighting operation, Nike initially made this statement:

> Nike is concerned by the serious and highly disturbing allegations made against Michael Vick and we consider any cruelty to animals inhumane and abhorrent. We do believe that Michael Vick should be afforded the same due process as any citizen, therefore, we have not terminated our relationship. We have, however, made the decision to suspend the release of the Zoom Vick V and related marketing communications. Nike will continue to monitor the situation closely and has no further comment at this time.[17]

Nike succumbed further to the continued pressure of animal-rights activists by eventually suspending its lucrative contract with Vick.

Vick, who was the top draft pick by the Atlanta Falcons in 2001 and once one of the wealthiest football players, was handed a 23-month sentence. He was convicted in August 2007 on charges of conspiracy and running a dog-fighting operation and suspended indefinitely from the NFL.[18]

Skoloda says the Woods and Vick situations have both similarities and differences.

> They both involve abuse. One might even think that spousal and family abuse by prolonged infidelity is even more heinous than animal abuse. But, Tiger was at the top of his game, while

Michael Vick is escorted from the Sussex County Courthouse in Virginia in 2008 after pleading guilty to charges involving dog fighting. He left prison in May 2009 to begin home confinement. (AP Photo/ Steve Helber, file)

Michael Vick was great, but not the greatest. Furthermore, the public outcry against Vick was so loud and decisive that Nike had to respond. With the Tiger Woods situation, infidelity is decried, but unfortunately seems to be all too common and the public has not blasted Tiger for his transgressions as they did Michael Vick.

After serving his time and being released from home confinement in July 2009, Vick began to work his way back into the NFL as most people knew he would. The Philadelphia Eagles signed him to a one-year, $1.6-million deal with the option for a second year, during which time he would earn $5.2 million, according to information provided by sources close to ESPN's Chris Mortensen.

"I just hope the people will understand that we did our research," Eagles Team President Joe Banner told the *Philadelphia Daily News*. "It was very tough initially, but everybody we talked to said the same thing—that he was remorseful and that he had gone through an incredible transformation, that he was basically good at heart. We heard this over and over again from people who felt he deserved a second chance."[19]

Vick later accepted blame in a *60 Minutes* interview for not stopping the illegal dog-fighting operation that he had bankrolled. He further stated that he feels tremendous hurt regarding what happened. When asked if he was more concerned about his football career or the dogs he hurt, he replied, "Football doesn't even matter."

Many animal lovers are inclined to think Vick is not being honest. Rather, he is remorseful only because he got caught and as far as football, it means the world to him. Doubt persists that he cares about the innocent dogs that were killed as a result of his conduct. Members of the People for the Ethical Treatment of Animals (PETA) agree with these sentiments and continue to remind football fans of why Vick went to prison. PETA Spokesman Dan Shannon comments,

> PETA and millions of decent football fans around the world are disappointed that the Eagles decided to sign a guy who hung dogs from trees. He electrocuted them with jumper cables and held them under water. You have to wonder what sort of message this sends to young fans who care about animals and don't want them to be harmed.[20]

Eagles Coach Andy Reid responded to the PETA remarks by saying, "This is America. We do make mistakes. This situation is a chance to prove he's doing the right things. He's been proactive speaking across the country."[21]

Nike became embroiled in a controversy about whether they had agreed to again sponsor Vick in late September 2009. Michael Principe, managing director of the BEST agency that represents Vick, announced during a Sports Sponsorship Symposium that Nike had signed a new deal with the newest member of the Eagles. Vick's agent, Joel Segal, also said Vick was looking forward to his relationship with Nike, although the terms of the deal were not going to be released.[22]

"He actually just became a Nike client," says Principe. "He has a new deal with Nike that we're all very pleased about."[23]

Nike countered with a statement the following morning saying the company does *not* have a contractual relationship with Vick. In the statement, the company said it has "agreed to supply product to Michael Vick as we do a number of athletes who are not under contract with Nike."[24]

It is difficult to determine exactly how Nike distinguishes between sponsoring athletes and just supplying products to them. However, it seems that a connection exists between the company and the athlete either way you define the relationship. Maybe the only difference is that Vick won't be featured in any Nike commercials at least for the time being.

In addition to making statements (or excuses) on behalf of athletes sponsored by the company, Nike is perpetually participating in the high-stakes game of creating new technology. Big-name endorsers and clever advertising campaigns certainly helped the company rise to power by making it a household name. However, the technology behind the products, going all the way back to the first prototypes and the early versions endorsed by Jordan, is the true reason why the company has stood the test of time. Even though I don't like trite, worn-out phrases, such as "stood the test of time," it really is the best way to describe Nike's longevity.

Chapter Seven

High-Tech Is High Stakes

Every time Nike designers go into the lab, a lot is riding on their creativity, scientific background, and thorough knowledge of the demands from professional athletes and customers. The company's climb to its current position in the industry was built upon solid research and development initiatives that have paid off tenfold with customer loyalty, name recognition, and a big-dollar return on investment.

Dirk DeCoy, co-owner of Strategin LLC, an Ohio-based corporation that provides technology and market assessments to evaluate the commercial potential of novel products, knows the critical role technology plays at a company like Nike. He notes,

> Incorporating technology into sporting apparel, equipment, and accessories is very important in obtaining increased sales, expanding product lines, and thriving in competitive markets. Technology plays a pivotal role in designing new products and even in the commercials advertising these products. People buying sporting apparel, equipment, and accessories are more than just consumers; they are what I call consumer-athletes. They perceive purchasing expensive sports apparel, equipment, and accessories as more like investing in themselves, rather than spending a hefty sum of money on a piece of equipment or a garment. They want products that will make them better, faster, and stronger than their competitors, whether they are competing against 30 runners in a race or just competing against themselves in a daily workout.

DeCoy brings to light the very real connection between today's savvy consumers and the need for companies to continually enhance the technological quality of their products. This connection is especially important to the consumer-athletes because winning gives them an unmatched sense of accomplishment. This mindset is a primary thrust behind the success of sporting goods companies. DeCoy has made many astute observations regarding this connection during his years in business.

He observes,

> You can correlate successful businesses with the age-old question of "Which came first—the chicken or the egg?" I firmly believe that the egg came first because chickens are afraid to do anything first. I correlate this to Nike because the company is very successful and has the capital to integrate new technologies into its product lines. Nike is not afraid to take the risks needed to become successful, or in other words the company is not afraid to be first in their market to introduce novel products.
>
>   Nike builds a product line, then informs or proves to the consumer-athletes via advertising and endorsements that they truly do need the product in order to be able to compete at a higher level. In essence, Nike moves the consumer-athletes to that higher level, rather than waiting for the consumer-athletes to realize they need the company's new products. One way they do this is by incorporating the latest technologies into their commercials.

DeCoy's comments regarding the use of technology in Nike's commercials would have fit easily into the chapter about the company's advertising campaigns. He explains how the company's high-tech commercials show action shots using slow-motion footage to create drama and exciting super-human feats created with the use of computer technology. Black-and-white commercials use technology to merge one bright color onto the film to make a particular product stand out as a beacon.

One of the most popular commercial formats uses multiple film clips of different athletes in action with motivational, ear-pounding music; and a brand name or symbol flashing throughout the commercial. Yet, not one word is spoken. Commercials based on nonverbal communications are perfect examples that prove actions speak louder than words, especially for consumer-athletes.

"Consumer-athletes need action and motivation to excite them. Technology helps intensify and create exciting action shots, dramatic images, and motivational rhythms that capture the consumer-athletes' attention to a point where they have to have the product to better their performance," explains DeCoy.

The consumer-athletes have plenty of opportunities to feed their desire for better performance by keeping track of Nike's latest products. As I began conducting research for this book, I was utterly amazed at how many products Nike has produced. The volume is astounding by itself, but the fact that each subsequent product is more sophisticated than the previous one is absolutely remarkable. I could have written a complete book just listing the products and explaining the technology that has been incorporated into each one.

As of December 2009, the company had just announced its Total90 Laser III interactive boot. By the time this book is published, many more products will have been released. The Total90 Laser III features a patent-pending Shot Shield strike zone designed specifically for enhanced power and accuracy. The boots, which actually look like colorful golf shoes, sell for about $200. Customers who purchase the boots receive a unique user code that provides online access to Nike Soccer+, which offers accuracy training drills and tutorials provided by the coaching experts at Juventus Football Club in Italy. The Nike+ digital experience provides a once-in-a-lifetime "signature move" training session taught by Fernando Torres, who plays for the Liverpool Football Club.

"I worked closely with the Nike design team on the Total90 Laser III and it definitely provides another dimension to my game and a greater feel for more accuracy, power, and swerve," Torres says. "What I like about the Nike Soccer+ system is that now every player can improve his skills with tips from myself and insights from top coaches on the pitch or on the go."[1]

The digital coaching experience that comes with the shoes can be accessed via the Web, the mobile Internet, or iPhone application to help players enhance their game skills. Customers can participate in the coaching program by visiting www.nikesoccer.com.

Although he may be a bit partial, Nike Soccer General Manager Bert Hoyt describes the latest innovation as the best performance boots available today. "But more than that, combining this technology with the Nike Soccer+ digital coaching program means you are not just buying a boot, you are buying a total game-improvement package."[2]

Information on the Nike Web site explains how designers broke down the biomechanics of striking the ball into specific elements to help them gain an in-depth understanding of the boot-to-ball relationship. They paid special attention to the instep and how players connect and put swerve on the ball. Their intense research resulted in a boot that delivers a cleaner strike on the ball for increased power, precision, and ball swerve at high velocity.

TECHNOLOGY BEHIND THE BOOT

The Total90 Laser III represents another page in the continual technology transformation that is synonymous with Nike. It was designed with the most modern, high-tech innovations, which are described on Nike's Web site as follows:

- Modular Instep: Five pods on the boot create a uniform contact point that creates a smoother surface for even pressure distribution. The pods are configured as five separate units that operate as one to remain flexible and fluid when interacting with the foot.
- Advanced shape-correcting memory foam: Provides a smooth and more consistent surface to enhance accuracy when shooting. This unique foam adapts to the demands of the individual player.
- Engineered Fins: Raised TPU (transparent thermoplastic urethane) fins on the medial side of the boot deliver increased friction on ball contact to ensure more swerve when needed. Each fin is strategically angled and sized to enhance control over ball trajectory, but folds on contact with the ball to accommodate great touch and feel.
- Reinforcements to the external heel counter and outsole increase comfort and stability.

STEVE NASH SUPPORTS CONSIDERED DESIGN

In addition to including the most technologically advanced design elements, Nike's recent product developments are mindful of the environment and the need to adhere to sustainability principles. Sports celebrities, who are also becoming quite vocal about environmental causes, are quick to endorse products that adhere to the latest buzzword of being "green." That is, of course, just another way to say the products are designed with nontoxic materials and manufactured in ways that are not harmful to the environment. As far back as 1993, long before the word "green" was popular, Nike started its Reuse-A-Shoe program. As part of the program, the company collects athletic shoes and grinds them into what it calls Nike Grind, the perfect name for a material used to make athletic tracks and courts.

Nike has tagged its environmentally friendly products under a banner called Considered Design, which has been lauded by the *International Design Magazine*. The Zoom MVP Trash Talk tennis shoes, which were released in a limited quantity on Earth Day in April 2009, epitomize the merger of performance and sustainability. The shoes, designed with Steve Nash of the Phoenix Suns in mind, are made from scrap materials generated from waste in the footwear manufacturing process.

Of all the many sports professionals I contacted while I was gathering information for this book, Nash responded the quickest. He actually took the time to answer the questions that I had emailed to

DC Headley, the basketball communications manager for the Phoenix Suns. Headley ranks at the top of my list of efficient people I have encountered as a journalist during the past two decades. In fact, I view him as an asset to the Phoenix Suns who is just as valuable to the team as its best basketball players.

Nash, who just happens to wear my favorite number 13 on his jersey, speaks passionately about environmental issues. Specifically, he believes:

> Sustainability should be important for everyone. We need to be considerate of our surroundings and our resources, and try to lessen the carbon footprint and the impact we have on the environment. For Nike to partner with me and create a shoe that sets an example not only in the industry, but also in a lifestyle for people to be more considerate of the Earth's resources is a step in the right direction. I thank them for taking a leadership role. It's important for people to continue using whatever possible lifestyle changes they can to renew, reuse, or recycle resources so we can really preserve the Earth.

Steve Nash, Phoenix Suns' guard, gets ready to shoot a free throw in a game against the Denver Nuggets in late 2009. (AP Photo/ David Zalubowski)

The Zoom MVP Trash Talk shoe belongs in Nike's Considered Design category because it epitomizes the principles of "renew, reuse, and recycle" that are important to Nash. For instance, the shoe laces are made from 100-percent recycled polyester, the sock liners are made from recycled foam rubber, and the upper and outsole include recycled leather and environmentally preferred rubber.[3]

Even the shoeboxes are constructed from 100-percent recycled fiber. Nike introduced its first recycled boxes in 1995, but the newer version has reduced the fiber content by about 30 percent. The company plans to use the Considered Design shoeboxes for all of its footwear styles beginning in 2011. It is estimated that converting to the new boxes will mean an annual savings of approximately 12,000 metric tons of cardboard, which is the astonishing equivalent of 200,000 trees.[4]

The company has announced its commitment to design all footwear to meet the baseline Considered Design standards by 2011, all apparel by 2015, and all equipment by 2020. Accomplishing this objective would translate to reducing waste in Nike's supply chain by 17 percent and increasing the use of environmentally preferred materials by 20 percent.[5] That is an ambitious goal, but Nike is known for being an overachiever in the world of athletic footwear. In addition to the Zoom MVP Trash Talk shoes, the AIR JORDAN XX3, as well as the AIR JORDAN 2009 and 2010 versions, meet the Considered Design standards.

Nash is proud of his association with the athletic footwear giant for many reasons. When asked what qualities Nike possesses that make him want to endorse the company's products, he said, "They make cool gear and that's the bottom line." He later elaborated and even talked about his earliest memories of wearing Nike shoes.

"I dreamed of endorsing their products. The first pair of tennis shoes I got was a John McEnroe pair and my first basketball shoes, I think, were the black and blue AIR JORDANs," he recalls. "I got those for Christmas one year, so that was one of the most memorable Christmas gifts I ever got."

For the past 14 years, Nash has enjoyed an affiliation with Nike that feels like a family relationship. It was an easy choice for him to endorse the Zoom MVP Trash Talk shoes. He explains,

> If you're somebody who feels a sense of responsibility to the planet, you are always looking for ways to impact the planet positively, so for me to marry my sport and my performance shoe with an environmental cause is a fantastic way to build a team that can make a change. The Considered Design products have kept me comfortable on the court and allowed me to train hard, play hard, and realize my goal. It's been a great partnership and, hopefully, one that can continue forever.

Nash has a strong opinion about why Nike has been able to influence the world of sports with such force.

"They have always pushed the envelope as far as creating products that are performance-based combined with great design not only for performance, but also for aesthetics," he says. "If a company is a leader aesthetically and functionally, they are going to change the game."

To say that Nike has changed the game is actually the understatement of the century. At times, the products and the athletes who endorse them receive so much attention that the sport takes a back seat. This is exactly what we talked about earlier when we explored the controversy surrounding Woods, Williams, and Vick.

PUSHING THE ENVELOPE FOR INNOVATION

Nash is right on the mark when he describes Nike as a company that has always pushed the envelope. Perhaps "pushing the envelope" will one day win the same acclaim as "Just Do It," if company leaders ever adopt it as a slogan. *Fortune* magazine regularly lists Nike in its rankings of the most admired companies for innovation. For a sports apparel and equipment company to be recognized for the use of innovation on the same list that is usually topped by corporations like Apple that do nothing but create technology certainly is noteworthy.

In 1999, Nike was asked to push the envelope to such a great extent and within such a tight deadline that it seems unfathomable to realize the company successfully completed the job. Officials from Sydney asked the company to sponsor the Australian Olympic team, giving the company less than eight months to design and produce more than 122,000 individual pieces of apparel. The overwhelming magnitude of the job becomes clear when you discover that the normal timeline from apparel design to delivery is typically 18 months. The company pushed its performance to the limit and achieved what some thought might be an impossibility.[6] The story is almost as uplifting as the accounts of athletes who push their performance to the limit and break all boundaries. Well, almost, but not quite.

In order for Nike to continue pushing the envelope, it is sometimes necessary to solicit the expertise of outside organizations. The company's long-range vision calls for all products to one day be designed as part of a closed-loop process, meaning they are created using the least amount of materials and can easily be recycled. To meet this goal, Nike has sought assistance from The Natural Step, an international nonprofit organization dedicated to education and research in sustainable development.

"The Natural Step and Nike have been working together to create a more sustainable future for 10 years," says The Natural Step Founder

Dr. Karl-Henrik Robert. "Nike's progress has been tremendous. We are proud to be partners in their journey."[7]

Richard Blume, senior advisor with The Natural Step, says Nike has distinguished itself as an innovator by incorporating sustainability into its design standards. "By using sustainability principles to guide decisions and create their Considered [Design] vision, Nike has ensured that its innovation efforts are informed by a rigorous, scientific understanding of sustainability. I have been inspired by Nike's commitment and leadership."[8]

Nike's formal research and development can be traced back to 1978 when Frank Rudy, a former aerospace engineer, worked with the company to create the first Air Sole units. These units were durable bags filled with pressurized gas that compressed under impact and then sprang back. A year later, this technology was used in the Tailwind, the first running shoe that featured Nike Air, the patented Air Sole cushioning system. The Air Force I, which hit stores in 1982, was the first basketball shoe to include the Nike Air technology, which employed the use of relatively novel computer-aided design techniques.

The company's Exeter research-and-development facility, which featured a sophisticated biomechanics shoe testing facility, opened in 1980 in New Hampshire. It was the precursor to the Nike Sports Research Lab located at the company headquarters in Beaverton, Oregon.

The technology being created by what was still a young company was becoming popular among athletes around the world who insisted on wearing high-performance, unique products. When Joan Benoit broke the women's world marathon record in 1983, she did it while wearing Nike shoes. Four months later, 23 Nike-supported athletes captured medals in the inaugural World Track and Field Championships in Helsinki, Finland.[9]

Since then, countless Nike-sponsored athletes have achieved accolades and won fame. I think these people would have been exceptional athletes even if they were wearing cheap, no-name tennis shoes. Let's face it. Michael Jordan would still have made the incredible shots without wearing the famous shoes, and Derek Jeter would make great plays for the New York Yankees no matter what type of shoes are on his feet. The technology and the products do not make the athletes. However, Nike's technology apparently makes their sporting efforts more comfortable and improves their performance to some degree.

The Nike Triax Sports Watch, developed in 1997, was described by *BusinessWeek* as a product that actually improved the sport of running. I wondered how a watch could receive such high praise and be described as an instrument for enhancing a runner's performance. This curiosity prompted me to conduct additional research to learn why the watch was so special.

I discovered that the Triax, which had been created with assistance from ASTRO Design Studios in Palo Alto, California, had a striking impact on the marketplace. The oval-shaped watch was featured on the cover of the November 29, 1999, edition of *BusinessWeek* with a headline that read "Best Selling Products of the Decade." *BusinessWeek* and the Industrial Designers Society of America (IDSA) had given the watch the nod for top honors among all products created in the 1990s.[10]

IDSA officials described the watch as a "coveted everyday mens-wear item" and "a brilliant example of how expertise and creative design can diversify a company's product line."[11]

BusinessWeek included information in that particular 1999 edition to explain why the watch was worthy of such recognition. The magazine article stated,

> Nike expanded its sports performance brand into a new area through great product design. Along the way, it actually im-proved the sport of running. The Triax watch is easy to read while jogging thanks to an oversize display. Nike launched it in November 1998 and sold $120 million (worth) in 18 months.[12]

Music has also found its way into the company's technology with the Nike SportMusic store on iTunes. Launched in 2006, the "store" is a destination for athletes searching for inspirational music and audio coaching. The coaching workouts provide guidance from celebrity ath-letes, including Lance Armstrong and Serena Williams, with music from artists like De La Soul and the group known as OK Go. De La Soul recently released its first original material in five years as part of a collaboration with Nike. The song "ARE YOU IN? Nike+Original Run" was written specifically with runners in mind, but the hip-hop music has mass appeal for a broad range of fans.

SPECIAL DESIGN ELEMENTS

The types of technology employed in the company's footwear and apparel can be divided into various categories, including Aerographics, Lunarlite Foam, Nike Swift, Flywire, and PreCool Technology.

Aerographics

The technology known as Aerographics is an engineered mesh design where up to half of the yarn in a garment can be removed. Unlike typical mesh shirts where a panel is added and additional seams are created, Aerographics incorporates the mesh directly into the garment without adding extra materials. This particular technology reduces the amount of material to produce more lightweight products, while adding comfort and passive cooling to the garment. The cooling effect is an important consideration for performance apparel in basketball, as well as track and field.

Aerographics was the brainchild of designer Kirk Meyer, who was researching ways to provide passive cooling without adding seams. The design creates a natural convection flow, pulling heat away from the body to cool the athletes. Aerographics has made it possible for designers to add country-specific graphic designs to the apparel. The graphic renderings can be transformed into zone-venting mesh that creates a cooling effect.

Lunarlite Foam Technology

This technology had its origins in the waffle sole created by Bowerman way back in the 1970s, although I doubt he knew that his early innovation would evolve to such a degree. Nike's historical information states that an employee made an interesting comment in 1971 when he tried the waffle shoe. "It was like running on pillows." When company designer Kevin Hoffer read the employee's quote in 2004, he began searching for a cushioning system that would mimic the same feeling.

Hoffer took into consideration the Moon Shoe, which featured the waffle sole. Believe it or not, he also found Internet information about the actual lunar landing and began downloading images of the astronauts bouncing around on the moon. The inspiration led to innovation.

Unfortunately, the Lunarlite foam was expensive and difficult to manufacture because the material was hard to stabilize and had a tendency to shrink. After the foam was blown into a form, it had to be quickly frozen to maintain its shape. Hoffer and Nike's Advanced Materials Team experimented and began filling freezers with foam wedges that resembled ice cream bars. The team eventually adjusted the compound's formula and began embedding it in phylon, with a foam pillow waffle outside that paid homage to the Lunar's original inspiration.[13] The phylon is made from foam pellets that are compressed, expanded with heat, and then cooled in a mold.

The foam has been applied to the LunarRacer, a performance shoe for distance running; the LunarTrainer for everyday running; the Hyperdunk lightweight basketball shoes; and the Nike Zoom Court Luna, which weighs half as much as a typical tennis shoe.

Tests performed on the original LunarRacer showed that the pressure load had a larger distribution area across the foot because the soft foam spreads the force evenly over a larger area, so athletes are not applying all of their pressure in one place. This feature protects the foot's bones and helps relieve pressure on the legs. Runners report having more energy in their races and requiring shorter recovery times.

The patented Lunarlite foam seemed like a logical choice when 2009 French Open winner Roger Federer approached Nike about designing a pair of stellar shoes to complement his style of tennis. The foam and a carbon-fiber shank in the middle of the sole support Federer's arches. The top part of the shoe is stabilized by Nike's Flywire technology, which we will discuss later in the chapter. Nike designs shoes for both Federer and his chief competitor, Rafael Nadal. The only difference is that the shoes are created with power in mind for Nadal and with a focus on speed for Federer, who incidentally is now tied with Pete Sampras for winning the most major tennis titles.[14]

Nike Swift

Nike is about more than footwear with apparel, sports equipment, and accessories also bringing in their share of annual revenue. The Advanced Innovation Team has invested a substantial amount of time to create apparel that provides athletes with an aerodynamic flair called the Swift System of Dress. The concept is to provide runners with gloves, socks, and arm coverings that will reduce wind resistance and, therefore, increase speed. The gloves feature dimpled fabrics to cut wind resistance and allow the arms to move through the air faster. The design team conducted tests that revealed the sleeves reduce drag by 19 percent and the socks by 12.5 percent.

The Nike Swift unitard features the Aerographics cooling system and is made from recycled polyester yarns that have been reclaimed not only from fabric, but also from soda bottles, consumer uniforms, and post-industrial fibers. Athletes wearing the Swift apparel in track and field, swimming, cycling, and speed skating have garnered more than 75 medals and 25 world records, according to information on Nike's Web site.

Company designers began developing the Swift apparel prior to the 2000 Olympic games in Sydney, Australia. They created the Aeromatrix wind tunnel and have tested more than 200 fabrics. The tunnel enables designers to analyze fabrics at wind speeds up to 100 miles per hour. Researchers can then categorize each type of fabric based on a precise testing protocol to guarantee the selected materials have the best performance characteristics. As a result of this comprehensive process, the designers can determine which fabric is best for each sport and various parts of the body. The Swift singlet and short, usually worn during sprinting and hurdling events, give athletes an alternative to wearing the full-body unitard. The tank shirt and shorts fit like a second skin just as the unitard does.[15]

PreCool Technology

Nike's original PreCool Vest has been redesigned to keep athletes cooler for a longer time by being lighter, fitting better, and being refillable. Company research shows that 25 percent of a body's total energy is consumed by moving muscle, while the other 75 percent is used to regulate heat. The vest cools the body's core temperature, helping athletes preserve their energy for the times they need it the most. Designers found inspiration in an unlikely source—a clingy black dress covered with tiny metal discs.

The revamped vest fits close to the body with large aluminum-coated triangles covering the back and stomach, and smaller ones being used to hug curves. Each triangle consists of two layers, one is filled with ice and the outer layer provides insulation. The aluminum reflects radiant heat while working like the coating on mirrored sunglasses. The outer layer and the aluminum coating have reduced the need for ice. The design team also created sealed compartments, modeled after leak-proof packaging used in the medical industry, that athletes can fill and freeze before competition.[16]

MOVING INTO THE 21ST CENTURY

Nike created the ultimate in foot comfort by utilizing a revolutionary approach to address fit, comfort, and sizing. The result was a lightweight running shoe that came in a variety of unusual sizes, including extra-extra small (XXS), extra small (XS), and small (S). This "t-shirt for your feet," as the company playfully tagged it, was known as Nike Air Presto.

Nike's researchers must be daredevils in the design room. Innovation continued in 2000 with the launching of Nike Shox, featuring a drastically different cushioning technology using materials from the engine mounts of cars. Never before had designers been bold enough to experiment by using engine mounts to provide stability and spring-like pillars of resistance in an athletic shoe.

Fast Company magazine printed an online story in late 2009 that raised an interesting point about cushioning systems. According to *Fast Company*, the inventors of the On Running Shoe, too much cushioning may be bad for a runner's feet. The On Shoe, which debuted in 2010, has a sole that collapses on impact to provide cushioning, but with the added benefit of shock absorber teeth that lock when fully compressed to offer a solid base for runners.[17] This is not a novel idea, however, and Nike probably has a shoe designed to fit the needs of even the most finicky runner.

THE LATEST NIKE SHOE TECHNOLOGY

The Nike Free was released in 2005, giving runners lightweight shoes with the sensation of running barefoot and strengthening their legs at the same time. The following year, customers were introduced to the Air Max 360, which was billed as "the most dramatic and compelling presentation of Nike Air cushioning ever." The shoe's foamless midsole was possible using a new method of creating Air-Sole units called thermoforming to emulate the effect of running on nothing, but air. In this case, I guess it would be Nike Air.

THE WONDER OF FLYWIRE

It is a bit deceiving when Nike refers to its latest creation as the lightest footwear ever because it seems that every subsequent version is described in the same manner. Just before the 2008 Olympics, the Flywire shoe was released along with the traditional description: "most innovative and lightest footwear." The description may be most appropriate in this case, though, because it is based on the revolutionary technology that uses high-strength threads to place support exactly where the foot needs it the most. Nike claims the Flywire and the Lunarlite technologies have reduced the weight of footwear by up to 18 percent.

Jay Meschter, innovation director of Nike's so-called Innovation Kitchen where the magic of creation occurs, explains,

> Flywire gets to that elusive thing of the plate just attaching to the bottom of the foot and forgetting about the shoe. It also gets Nike one step closer to achieving one of Bill Bowerman's goals. When he was a coach, he said the ideal track spike would be a nail through the foot. With Flywire, it's not quite as extreme as a nail, but it's as close as anyone has gotten to applying a spike plate directly to feet.[18]

The paper-thin shoe is only about two microns thick and is supported by threads that act like the cables on a suspension bridge. The amount of material required for the upper of the shoe has been drastically reduced to a bare minimum. In addition, the track spikes now weigh less than 100 grams, a weight never before used without compromising durability and support.

Flywire was more than six years in the making until Meschter and his team could find the necessary machinery and processes to deliver the technology in a cost-effective manner. Remarkably, the solution to what seemed like such a monumental obstacle was located right in one of Nike's research buildings. It was an embroidery machine that eventually was reprogrammed to produce the type of stitches that were necessary to support the technology.

The unusual creative process soon began to unfold with collaboration between the design team and the biomechanics experts in Nike's Sports Research Lab. The designers' feet were wrapped up to the heel with duct tape to provide lateral support. Using the team members' feet as part of the process, researchers were able to determine where the Flywire fibers had to be positioned in order to be the most effective. The placement of the filaments makes the uppers feel more like a second skin with the threads providing all of the support and preventing slippage, a problem that was previously considered unsolvable.

If the shoe truly does prevent slippage and is so incredibly light, perhaps it can make the difference between winning or losing that big race.

GOLF INNOVATIONS

Nike Golf announced in December 2008 that it was making the same "game-changing technology" used by professionals available to consumers. The STR8-FIT (pronounced just like it looks, straight fit) technology in the company's SQ DYMO STR8-FIT and the SQ DYMO² (square shaped) drivers features eight club-head positions. Nike claims these positions can "dramatically or subtly perfect ball flight," making the drivers the first of their kind on the market.

Tom Stites, Nike Golf's director of club creation, says,

I have worked on a number of great products in my time, but never has there been a product that allows a golfer to change his or her results so quickly and effectively. The new SQ DYMO STR8-FIT and SQ DYMO² STR8-FIT drivers allow the golfer to change the face and shaft relationship up to plus or minus two degrees for face angle, loft, and lie. Nothing influences ball flight more than face, loft, and lie angles. This is significant because it means that if a player normally hits the ball far right or left, there is at least one of the eight locations of the STR8-FIT that will allow him or her to hit in or near the fairway. And straight equals greater distance.[19]

Nike Golf officials say the drivers, which are available at a manufacturer's suggested retail price of $540, have proven their worth on the PGA Tour. For example, Trevor Immelman achieved his first major championship victory at the Masters Golf Tournament using this technology in 2008. Other professional golfers who used the drivers were K. J. Choi, the first to win with the technology at the Sony Open in January 2008; and Anthony Kim, who was victorious at the Wachovia Championship and the AT&T Classic.

Nike describes the STR8-FIT technology on its Web site as "an innovation that provides golfers with the opportunity to hit the ball longer and straighter by changing the head position." It continues,

Simple changes can be made before their round to dramatically correct their ball flight or subtly perfect it through the selection of eight unique head positions from open to close with one club, eliminating the use of multiple shafts and movable weights. This is a new and unique way for each individual consumer to control his or her own game, much like the Nike tour athletes use the Nike Tour Van at tournament sites prior to a round to adapt their equipment for the day's round.

If a golfer is pushing, fading, or slicing the ball too much and they wish to draw the ball or hit more to the left for a particular course set up, they can change the position of their clubface to a more closed position. If a golfer is hooking, pulling, or drawing the ball more than they wish, they can manually change the clubface to a more open position. Clubface angles range from a neutral position of zero degrees to both one and two degrees closed or open.

The Nike Tour Van and the assistance it provides to professional golfers served as the inspiration for the new drivers. The van is equipped with a staff of Nike club experts who are capable of adjusting the driver to a precise face and lie angle needed for the most optimal performance.

As far back as 2000, Nike saw a hike in sales of its golf apparel and equipment after Woods switched to the Nike Precision Tour Accuracy golf balls, which were first introduced as an innovation in 1998. The first company golf clubs with forged blade irons, forged wedges, and forged titanium drivers were available at retail locations in 2002. The clubs pushed Nike Golf up the ladder as a formidable player in golf footwear, apparel, and equipment. Innovative clubs include the Slingshot irons and the SasQuatch driver.

DeCoy, the business owner who gave his perspective on Nike's technology earlier in this chapter, is also an avid golfer. He used to believe that golfers could make any equipment work, if they possessed the proper athletic ability and sufficient coordination to hit the ball just right. He was never a believer in the notion that the brand of equipment actually makes a difference in how well a golfer plays. That is, until recently.

During a golf outing in South Bend, Indiana, DeCoy's friend asked if he wanted to try his new driver. DeCoy initially declined, but later agreed upon the insistence of his golf buddy. The more technologically advanced driver made it easier to drive the ball a lot straighter and a little longer, and was more forgiving of mistakes in his swing.

DeCoy notes,

The technology incorporated into that one driver made me a better golfer. I am now convinced that the equipment makes the golfer and I know this is true of other sports, as well. Compound this by 13 other clubs in my golf bag, all containing the latest technology regarding balance, material and weight, and you can see how a golfer's game could be dramatically improved with each club, with each stroke.

DeCoy refers to his friend as one of the consumer-athletes he has described—someone who could talk endlessly about the purchase of his new golf clubs.

"The consumer-athletes like to compete in the business world and in the recreational world. They will spend a hefty amount of money on technology that will make them better, faster, stronger," says DeCoy. "They need to compete and they need the satisfaction of winning or improving their performance."

DeCoy did not divulge whether the new clubs purchased by his friend were made by Nike or another company. I guess it doesn't matter, though, because Nike has already scored a hole in one with its golf innovations.

DRESSED FOR PERFECTION

The company's technology is carefully woven not only into all of its footwear and equipment, but also into its apparel. Nike expends a significant amount of time and effort to ensure that athletes like Woods are outfitted properly.

More than a year before Woods competed in the 138th British Open in 2009, he met with Nike designers to determine what clothes he would be wearing in the competition. Nike and other companies that make sports apparel know that outfitting the top athletes is big business. Every time Woods won a competition, it was a sure bet that his picture would be shown around the world on television, in print, and via electronic formats for many weeks to come. Publicity of that magnitude equates to more free advertising for the apparel companies. The clothes worn by Woods for the British Open, the U.S. Open, the Masters, and the PGA Championship have been designed specifically for him to wear on these particular days. Of course, Woods and the other elite athletes in this category have input into the look they will sport.

"Tiger won't wear white pants, for example, and he won't wear green pants," says Doug Reed, the global director of golf apparel and accessories for Nike. He adds,

One year, we proposed he wear a dark green shirt on a Saturday at the PGA Championship. Tiger took one look at it and said, "The PGA is in Oklahoma in August. There's no way. I'm not wearing a dark shirt in that heat." When someone has the lead and you see him on television walking up to the final green, you can't help but think back to a year ago when you first showed him that shirt and pants. It's a thrill when somebody wins wearing your stuff. When Tiger debuts a new red shirt, it sells because let's face it. Everyone wants to play golf like Tiger.[20]

Nike puts a lot of effort into designing the clothes that will be worn by athletes associated with the company. A special event was staged last summer in Manhattan, an appropriate location as the company unveiled its New York-inspired U.S. Open apparel and footwear for tennis players Roger Federer, Rafael Nadal, Serena Williams, and Maria Sharapova. The company built a temporary, yet regulation-size, tennis court just to showcase the products with appearances by tennis legend John McEnroe, as well as Federer, Nadal, and Williams.

"We are very proud to raise the bar for this year's U.S. Open apparel and footwear collection by drawing inspiration from New York's style and energy," says Janice Lucena, global tennis design director for Nike. "From Nadal's taxi cab yellow polo to the sleek sophistication of Maria and Serena's night dresses, we continue to create product that helps our athletes perform better on the court while looking incredible."[21]

Nike added a community outreach component to this unveiling by providing opportunities for fans to receive inspirational tips from the tennis pros and giving various youth organizations a chance to win donations. Without the community outreach focus, it would have been just downright blatant self-promotion.

"This is an exciting opportunity to bring the thrill of the U.S. Open directly to tennis fans in New York," said McEnroe. "Providing a platform for kids to experience the beauty and power of this game and meet their tennis icons is incredible."[22] McEnroe proclaimed himself as an icon, but I would have expected nothing less from him.

Those in attendance were treated to colorful exhibits to showcase the clothing. The most noteworthy fact was that Nike has included its Dri-FIT fabric in the apparel to enhance comfort, while keeping the athletes cool and dry on the court.

Keeping the athletes warm and comfortable was the objective when Nike designed the apparel for members of the U.S. Olympic and Paralympic teams for the 2010 Winter Games in Vancouver, Canada. The Team USA Medal Stand Collection includes head-to-toe Nike outfitting that boasts performance features, technological innovations, and the company's Considered Design sustainable elements.

"Our designers combined performance benefits and sustainability, while infusing a modern approach with classic old-school styles," says Scott Williams, Nike's creative director of innovation/Olympics. "The result is the best of all worlds. We've created our warmest, ultra-lightweight,

Tennis legend John McEn-
roe returns a shot to his
opponent Diego Nargiso of
Italy in the U.S. Open in
New York in 1992. (AP
Photo/Bebeto Matthews)

most waterproof and breathable Olympic apparel ever, all through a sustainable lens."[23]

The Considered Design products use environmentally preferred materials and minimize waste throughout the entire design and development process. The products, which are available at select retailers, in Niketown stores, and online at www.Nikestore.com and www.Team USAShop.com, include a waterproof down jacket made from 100-percent recycled polyester; waterproof pants; and the Air Blazer ACG footwear, which combines 1970s street style with the high performance of an outdoor trail shoe.

"The Team USA Medal Stand look demonstrates Nike's ability to blend performance and innovation with new sustainable features," notes Lisa Baird, the U.S. Olympic Committee's chief marketing officer. "We couldn't be more pleased with the products Nike has presented for our athletes, and we appreciate their leadership and dedication to the sustainability of their products."[24]

Sustainability is just one of many areas in which the company focuses its intention in terms of being a good corporate leader.

Chapter Eight

Serving as a Role Model

The awards Nike has earned for various reasons, including its sustainability efforts, pale in comparison to the amount of money and attention the company has garnered for its pioneering products and captivating commercials. Nonetheless, these achievements are worth highlighting to show the company is receiving recognition from organizations that believe it is doing a superior job in so many other arenas.

In 2009, the company received a myriad of awards to recognize its commitment to corporate responsibility, ethics, sustainability, and climate. We will delve into each one of these categories separately, but first, I want to share some of President and CEO Mark Parker's thoughts on corporate responsibility. According to him, Nike can play a vital role in contributing to a positive transformation throughout the world by effecting social and environmental changes. The company reviewed its corporate responsibility policies in 2005–2006 and has been implementing incremental improvements since then.

Parker elaborates on the company's philosophy regarding corporate responsibility:

> We see corporate responsibility as a catalyst for growth and innovation, an integral part of how we can use the power of our brand, the energy and passion of our people, and the scale of our business to create meaningful change. Corporate responsibility at Nike has grown beyond its role as a tool to define, discover and address compliance issues, or to manage risk and reputation. Today, corporate responsibility no longer exists on the periphery as a check on our business, but is assuming its rightful role as a source of innovation within our business. Corporate responsibility is no longer a staff function at Nike. It's a design function, a sourcing function, a consumer-experience function, part of how we operate.
>
> Nike is competitive. We don't want to get better; we want to win. If real change is to occur in our supply chain and contract

factories, in the communities in which we operate, and in the broader world we influence, then small steps will always fall short of our potential. Big goals are needed to realize big achievements. So we've set a series of strategic business targets for ourselves that are aggressive, but achievable, by fiscal year 2011.[1]

Parker's report on corporate responsibility lists three primary areas where the company intends to focus its efforts in order to achieve its business targets by fiscal year 2011. These areas include:

- Improving working conditions in the contract factories via a holistic, integrated business approach to the supply chain;
- Minimizing the company's global environmental footprint through sustainable product innovation and supply chain innovation in direct operations and contract factories; and
- Using the power of the brand to provide greater access to the benefit of sports for youths around the globe. The company regularly invests millions of dollars to establish or support community-based sports initiatives.

The company has already taken significant steps, leading the way with its Considered Design philosophy toward sustainability. Targets are being met for reducing waste, eliminating volatile organic compounds, and increasing the use of environmentally friendly materials in the design and packaging of products. Parker explains,

> As Nike innovation proves what's possible in sustainable product design, we'll raise our standards. Our footprint impacts millions of people directly and indirectly each year. Our operations touch thousands of smaller businesses within multiple industries, all part of an established global trading system dependent on a host of other partners and all governed by the framework of a publicly traded company.
>
> We will leverage our business model, our products, our natural strengths, and our voice to be a vehicle for change. We believe that design and innovation can deliver the most valuable solutions. We believe that entrepreneurship is the best source for sustainable solutions. We believe that now is the time to seek and create radical collaborations between global businesses, social entrepreneurs and activists, governments, non-governmental organizations, and civil society. Everybody has part of the answer."[2]

Numerous organizations have taken note of Nike's efforts to be a good corporate citizen and environmental steward. The company was included on the list of 100 Best Corporate Citizens for 2009 by *Corporate Responsibility Officer* (*CRO*) magazine. Three companies—Intel, Cisco, and Starbucks—have made it on the list all 10 years that *CRO* has been compiling the data. Topping the 2009 list was Bristol-Meyers Squibb, and the 26th spot was occupied by Nike.[3]

The CRO list takes into consideration the contenders' performance in the key areas of environment, climate change, human rights, employee relations, philanthropy, financial, and governance. We have talked about several of these areas as they pertain to Nike, but we will discuss climate change, human rights, sustainability, and overall corporate responsibility to a greater extent as we move through this chapter.

Nike was included among the 99 honorees on the 2009 list of the "World's Most Ethical Companies." The list is compiled by the Ethisphere Institute, a New York–based international think tank devoted to the creation, advancement, and sharing of best practices pertaining to business ethics, anti-corruption, social responsibility, and sustainability.

Nominations are submitted to Ethisphere each year from companies around the world who want to earn their spot on the list. In 2009, nominations poured in from companies representing 35 industries in more than 100 countries. The scoring methodology was developed by Ethisphere with assistance from a committee of top-rated attorneys, government officials, professors, and organization leaders. Companies that submit a nomination must complete an in-depth survey and then are judged on a variety of categories. Corporate citizenship and responsibility account for 20 percent of the score; legal, regulatory, and reputation track record, 20 percent; innovation that contributes to public well-being, 15 percent; executive leadership and tone from the top, 15 percent; internal systems and ethics/compliance programs, 15 percent; corporate governance, 10 percent; and industry leadership, 5 percent. The final selection of winners is based on the scoring from the survey results and the comprehensive analysis and research conducted by Ethisphere.[4]

Before being hailed as one of the world's most ethical companies, Nike enjoyed a triple-header of being named to *Fortune* magazine's list of "100 Best Companies to Work For" in 2006, 2007, and 2008. It was number 82 on the list in 2008, but slipped out of sight with no mention in 2009. The 2008 blurb about Nike states: "Four times a year, staff at the sports-crazed company are invited to an all-employee meeting. Those completing their 10th year are invited to the Decathletes Dinner."[5]

Company leaders have consistently stated over the past five years that they are achieving substantial positive changes for workers by taking the following steps:

- Eliminating excessive overtime in contract factories;
- Using human resources management systems, specifically in contract factories, which include training on workers' rights,

women's rights, and freedom of association and collective
bargaining;
- Transitioning to lean manufacturing processes; and
- Encouraging other brands to partner with the company so the
  supply chain will be monitored in collaboration with multiple
  stakeholders.

Being lauded for its corporate responsibility, ethics, and workplace
culture is a welcome improvement from last decade when the company was confronted with allegations of child labor and sweatshop
conditions at some of its factories. Knight made it onto another list in
1996, but the publicity was not quite as glowing as the more recent information about the company being commended for its ethical behavior and responsible governance.

Instead, he filled the third spot on a list of "corporate crooks,"
who were named in *Downsize This!* which was written by filmmaker
and outspoken political commentator Michael Moore. In the book and
subsequent film, *The Big One*, Moore made allegations about the atro-
cious working conditions and next-to-nothing wages in Indonesian
sweatshops, where pregnant women and teenage girls sewed shoes at
factories that were under contract to make the Nike products.

After word spread about the information contained in the book,
Knight agreed to be interviewed on camera by Moore. This was a
brave move, considering Moore had targeted executives at other companies as "crooks," and nobody else agreed to go on camera. In the
interview, which can be seen on youtube.com, Knight does not provide
many direct answers. He does describe Indonesia as "an underdevel-
oped country with a repressive regime" and states that "Americans do
not want to make shoes."[6]

Kelley Skoloda, the marketing expert who has given her opinion
throughout this book, says it is important for companies to make it
easy for consumers to learn about their business practices.

"Nike has suffered in this arena due to questionable business practices in product manufacturing," she says. "Any company that espouses
accomplishments at high levels must hold themselves to the same high
standards today."

On the heels of Moore's public stance against certain Nike business
practices, Knight vowed in 1998 to commit to more stringent standards
at the factories that make the company's products. The strict guidelines
pertain to minimum age requirements, air quality, factory monitoring,
mandatory education programs, and improved access to Nike's corporate responsibility practices.[7] In 2005, Nike was among the first companies in its industry to disclose the list of more than 700 factories that
make its products throughout the world.

The corporate responsibility details provided on Nike's Web site also include information regarding more recent allegations of child labor in Uzbekistan, a country in Central Asia. A statement on the site reads, "Nike takes very seriously reports of widespread use of forced child labor in Uzbekistan cotton production. We do not knowingly source cotton from Uzbekistan."[8]

The statement further explains that Nike has taken action to address the allegations. First, it enhanced monitoring to ensure that no cotton from Uzbekistan was unknowingly entering the supply chain. Next, it has participated in a network of brands, industry groups, investors, trade unions, and nongovernmental organizations in an effort to eradicate forced labor practices in Uzbekistan cotton production.

Despite being the subject of harsh headlines in the past, the company's "green" movement has been making the news much more often today than talk about child labor.

CONNECTING CORPORATE RESPONSIBILITY TO SUSTAINABILITY

Nike's leadership team is steadfast in its belief, and rightfully so, that corporate responsibility must include a plan for sustainability. The sustainability, in turn, will lead to ever-changing improvements in innovation and the production of more eco-friendly products. A special team has been created to drive sustainable business and innovation, which go hand-in-hand in today's economic and corporate climates. The Corporate Responsibility Department has taken advantage of the opportunity to restructure the team to further pursue innovative and sustainable business models for the future. The aim of this new team, now called Sustainable Business and Innovation, is to drive sustainability across all aspects of Nike.

Hannah Jones, vice president of this new group, says, "While Nike's commitment to the three key areas of factory working conditions, Considered Design and the environment, and sport for social change continues, the way in which we will be organized to achieve innovation and sustainable results for the business is evolving."[9]

As part of its evolving business model, the company is including sustainable design, engineering, and building principles in its facilities management, renovation, and new construction projects. For example, spot cooling and solar-tracking skylights are featured in the design of the company's Northridge Distribution Center in Memphis, Tennessee. In addition, retail facilities are conserving energy by using more efficient lighting and air conditioning systems. Energy-efficient measures implemented at the world headquarters in Oregon have earned the company the Energy Star rating from the U.S. Environmental Protection Agency.

The efforts have transcended the United States to be integrated into the company's European facilities. The European headquarters in the Netherlands uses a ground source heat pump and a daylight-harvesting system to curtail energy consumption, while the distribution center in Belgium has a densely insulated shell and pre-cooling system to better control the regulation of temperatures. Renewable energy sources, such as windmill power, are also being used. In fact, the Belgium distribution center is powered entirely by six on-site windmills.

The company has been working since 2001 to better understand what actions are necessary to reduce its environmental footprint throughout the entire process from the supply chain to the consumer. Important research has been conducted by partnering with four of its contract footwear manufacturing facilities in Vietnam and China. The research revealed that a footwear factory can contain more than 15,500 motors, 10,000 lightbulbs, 6,000 sewing machines, six separate chillers, and numerous large boilers, as well as four separate compressor farms. Nike has been using the research results to determine how it can optimize or reduce energy usage throughout its contract factories.[10]

The company's "green" work was recognized in 2009 by *NEWS-WEEK*, Corporate Knights, Inc., and Innovest Strategic Value Advisors. Nike did impressively well in the *NEWSWEEK* rankings, scoring seventh place on a list of 500 of the largest U.S. companies as measured by market capitalization, revenue, and number of employees.

NEWSWEEK compiled the list in collaboration with three research partners, including KLD Research & Analytics, which gathers environmental, social, and governance data on corporations throughout the world; Trucost, which focuses on environmental performance; and CorporateRegister.com, the world's largest online directory pertaining to social responsibility, sustainability, and environmental reporting. The *NEWSWEEK* information, released in September 2009, assigned a score to each company based on the three components of environmental impact, green policies, and reputation. The environmental impact aspect reflects the total cost of all environmental effects of a corporation's global operations. The green policies score was derived from an analytical assessment of each company's environmental policies and performance, taking into consideration best-in-class policies, programs and initiatives, community impact, and regulatory infractions. The reputation component is based on the results of an opinion survey completed by corporate social responsibility professionals, academic leaders, and environmental experts.[11]

While Nike placed seventh on the overall list, it came in first in the industry sector of consumer products with a "Green Score" of

93.2 percent. The following remarks relevant to Nike were offered in the *NEWSWEEK* listing:

> Leads its industry in environmental management of suppliers. Code of conduct requires over 650 contract factories in 52 countries to have written environmental policies. Initiatives include using organic cotton; its entire manufacturing process generates less waste than its retail packaging. Introduced a basketball shoe in 2009 made from environmentally preferred materials, such as recycled polyester, and packaging in a 100-percent recycled fiber box.[12]

Nike also earned a spot, along with 19 other U.S. companies, on the Global 100 list compiled in 2009 by Corporate Knights, Inc. and Innovest Strategic Value Advisors. The list of the most sustainable companies in the world was provided in alphabetical order rather than by rank in terms of which companies fared the best. Nike was in good company, being joined on the list by the following other domestic corporations: Advanced Micro Devices; Alcoa, Inc.; Amazon.com; Baxter International, Inc.; Coca-Cola; Dell, Inc.; Eastman Kodak Co.; FPL Group, Inc.; Genzyme Corp.; Goldman Sachs Group, Inc.; Hewlett-Packard Co.; Intel Corp.; PG&E Corp.; Pinnacle West Capital Corp.; Procter & Gamble Co.; Prologis; State Street Corp.; United Technologies Corp.; and Walt Disney Co. Adidas AG, the Germany-based sports apparel manufacturer, also appeared on the list. The winning companies are recognized each year at the Davos World Economic Forum in Switzerland.

"While markets go up and down, companies like the Global 100 members that prudently take care of the interests of all their stakeholders offer the best bet for society and investors in the long-term," says Toby Heaps, editor of *Corporate Knights* magazine. This particular magazine, published by the Canadian-based Corporate Knights media company, has the largest circulation of any publication focused solely on responsible business.[13]

The Global 100 project, launched in 2005, was initiated by Corporate Knights with research support from the New York-based investment advisory firm known as Innovest Strategic Value Advisors. The research provided by Innovest is invaluable to compiling the list because the company specializes in analyzing nontraditional factors that drive risk and shareholder value, including the performance of companies on environmental, social, and strategic governance issues.

"The continuing out-performance of the Global 100, even in the midst of the current global financial crisis, provides eloquent testimony and yet more evidence for investors, company executives, governments, and civil society alike," says Innovest CEO Matthew Kiernan. "Superior positioning and performance on environmental, social, and governance issues does provide a valuable leading indicator of best-managed, more agile, future-proof companies. We expect this sustainability premium to become even larger in the coming years."[14]

Kiernan's words "become even larger in the coming years" could have been used to describe Nike at any point in its history and could be used today to predict what the future will undoubtedly hold for the company. Being recognized on one list after another for sustainability is noteworthy, but it is nearly insignificant when compared to the company's other accomplishments for which it will always be best known. No matter how many initiatives are implemented to conserve resources and curtail emissions, Nike will never be known by the general public primarily for its sustainability.

In this age of environmental awareness, it is hard for any global company to make a decision without considering green options. The collective spotlight of social consciousness is ready to fault any company that does not make a stand to be more environmentally responsible. It's hard to find a company that has not taken even a few steps to be more green, even if it is something as simple and cost-effective as switching to more efficient lighting. It is a far more arduous task to find a company like Nike that has ascended to unprecedented heights from such meager beginnings.

"Green" had a whole different meaning to the Nike founders as they worked their way up the ladder to build a successful company, a journey that rewarded them with the color of money. It's hard to imagine that Nike never would have existed without the courage of Bowerman and Knight to chase their dreams. It seems like the company has always been in existence and that the sustainability efforts are serving the fine purpose of making it more efficient and robust as a global powerhouse.

Other organizations that are known as powerhouses for driving sustainability are ideal collaborators for Nike's green movement. In late 2009, the shoe giant became one of the first companies to partner with PopTech, a network of global leaders from numerous disciplines who explore the social impact of new technologies. The partnership will fuel the network's PopTech Labs, which will gather input from a select group of corporate leaders, scientific researchers, engineers, policy makers, and other stakeholders to study topics of value to business, society, and the environment. The first lab will explore the discovery of new green materials that can be used in closed-loop ecosystems, meaning the materials in the finished product could be recycled and used as input for new products. Other companies that have partnered with PopTech, which has offices in Maine and New York, include Microsoft, eBay, Target, and Lexus.[15]

Nike Considered Design General Manager Lorrie Vogel says Nike has made huge strides in designing more sustainable products, but the company cannot continue tapping into declining resources. "We have to unlock the power of collective innovation to create a future where you can literally turn an old shoe into a new shoe or an old shirt into a new shirt. That currently isn't possible because we don't have access to the ideal sustainable and recyclable materials to make these products in the first place."[16]

The closed-loop philosophy also applies to the GreenXchange undertaken by a nonprofit organization called Creative Commons in conjunction with Nike and Best Buy. Creative Commons, headquartered in San Francisco, is dedicated to expanding the amount of creative works that are available by providing a forum for others to build upon existing projects in a manner that is ethical and legal.

If you explore information about the initiative on the Internet, it sounds both complicated and ambiguous. However, the concept is actually quite simple. The partners work together to create a platform of open innovation and collaboration that encourages the sharing of ideas and the adoption of green technologies. In particular, the project is intended to establish strategies for using patents and industry expertise within a community network to promote innovation.

The mantra of the GreenXchange is "Close the loop. Grow the business." A booklet created by Creative Commons and Nike provides what they call "words to live and thrive by." The words are short and sweet, but could be effective if businesses take them to heart. "Imagination is infinite. Resources aren't. Act accordingly. Design products to be reused and reborn. Everything has a use. Waste nothing. Apply nothing to the product or process that harms. Seek fossil fuel independence."[17]

Capitol Hill has lauded Nike for being a leader in doing precisely what the GreenXchange proposes by collaborating with others and exploring options for sustainability. U.S. Sen. Gordon Smith, a Republican from the Nike home state of Oregon, recognized the company in remarks he made on the Senate floor in 2008. He explained to his fellow lawmakers:

> Nike is exporting their world-class products; they are also exporting the values of sustainability throughout the world as they continue their efforts to reduce the company's carbon footprint in contract manufacturing facilities in Asia. Nike has been a leader in developing sustainable products and components since its inception. Nike's legacy continues to grow as they lead the way as an extremely successful company, but not forgetting about how important it is to preserve and protect the natural resources around us.[18]

FIGHTING FOR CLIMATE CHANGE MEASURES

Some people might argue that Nike's involvement in social causes has a direct correlation to the company's yearning for publicity or a longing to shed the bad press about the child labor allegations. However, the company no longer needs to acquire attention to achieve industry milestones. It has already been there and done that. Somewhere along the way, perhaps after Knight became a billionaire, the company's executives realized they could use Nike's stature for the greater good and still be profitable.

The company has used its name recognition to lobby for change in Washington, D.C., by partnering with the World Wildlife Fund, Inc. (WWF) regarding climate change issues. In 2008, Nike was among 11 companies that joined the WWF in sending a letter to Congress urging lawmakers to support the Lieberman-Warner Climate Security Act. The proposed legislation, which had not reached fruition at the time I wrote this chapter, aimed to reduce the emissions of greenhouse gases in the United States by approximately 60 percent below 2005 levels by the year 2050.

The companies state in their letter:

> Our companies have long recognized that unchecked carbon emissions are resulting in large-scale climate change that threatens serious economic, social, and environmental consequences. We recognize that this is a global problem requiring a global response. As leading companies committed to demonstrating real action, we are working to reduce our collective climate impact. Many of our strategies have now become models for the growing number of businesses that are choosing to move to low-carbon business practices. We are working towards ambitious emissions-reduction targets, while demonstrating that improving energy efficiency and transitioning to clean energy are entirely compatible with improving business growth and shareholder value. Our companies recognize that ignoring climate change is not an option. What will ultimately undermine economic growth is a failure to take action.[19]

Nike and many of the same companies, along with the WWF, renewed their plea to Congress in September 2009 by again asking the Senate to pass comprehensive climate change legislation that would drastically reduce greenhouse emissions and encourage investment in technology innovations. The companies, which are part of the Climate Savers alliance that was formed a decade ago, cite scientific evidence that clearly shows the damaging impact the rapidly changing climate is having on wildlife, water resources, farms, forests, crops, and coastlines. The companies are trying to send a strong message illustrating that capping greenhouse gas emissions will unleash new business opportunities, level the playing field for domestic companies, and ensure that the U.S. economy can compete for clean energy in global markets. The theme for Climate Savers is simple, yet very telling: "Let the Clean Economy Begin."

U.S. Chamber of Commerce President and CEO Thomas Donohue has stated the chamber supports strong federal legislation and a binding international agreement to reduce carbon emissions and address climate change. However, he also stated that Congress should set climate change policy through legislation, rather than letting the U.S. Environmental Protection Agency (EPA) apply existing environmental statutes that were not intended to regulate greenhouse gas emissions.[20]

Among the corporations that took exception to the chamber's position regarding the EPA were Nike, Apple, and several power companies. Although Apple pulled its membership from the chamber, Nike retained its membership, but resigned from its position on the board of directors.

Nike officials justify their position regarding the chamber in this statement:

> We will continue our membership to advocate for climate change legislation inside the committee structure and believe that we can better influence policy by being part of the conversation. Moving forward, we will continue to evaluate our membership. We fundamentally disagree with the U.S. Chamber of Commerce on the issue of climate change, and their recent action challenging the EPA is inconsistent with our view that climate change is an issue in need of urgent action. It is important that U.S. companies be represented by a strong and effective chamber that reflects the interests of all its members on multiple issues. We believe that on the issue of climate change, the chamber has not represented the diversity of perspective held by the board of directors.[21]

Daily news accounts in the print and online media are laden with information about companies taking action and banding together to make a difference. The name Nike appears in many of the articles and, therefore, writing this book required me to conduct extensive research and to continually update my work. Being a former editor of a daily newspaper, I am accustomed to meeting tight deadlines and shifting gears quickly and seamlessly from one project to another. The news never stops happening and it appears as though Nike is perpetually increasing its stride toward excellence.

The company maintains a steady, full-steam-ahead pace, which I think is a very commendable quality for companies and individuals to possess. Keep moving forward no matter what obstacles you may encounter. Nike has never lost its "Just Do It" attitude. It just keeps pushing toward tomorrow by building on its successes and learning from its failures. Fortunately for Nike, the company rarely has endured what most would consider a failure. Company leaders are masters at collaborating with others to continually advance meaningful causes.

For example, the company worked with Ceres and four other corporations to start a new business coalition in 2009 to compel lawmakers to pass strong climate and energy legislation. Ceres, located in Boston, is a national network of environmental organizations, investors, and public interest groups that work with companies to address sustainability challenges. The Business for Innovative Climate and Energy Policy (BICEP) coalition started by these groups has established key objectives, which include, but are not limited to, promoting energy efficiency and green jobs, sparking interest in renewable energy, and limiting new coal-fired power plants to those capable of capturing and storing their carbon emissions. Nike outpaced other apparel companies to land the first-place spot on the Ceres' ranking of consumer and technology companies regarding climate change strategies.

"These companies have a clear message for next year's Congress— move quickly on climate change to kick-start a transition to a prosperous clean-energy economy fueled by green jobs," observes Ceres President Mindy Lubber.[22]

Sarah Severn, director of the Horizons corporate responsibility team at Nike, says the company felt that the powerful voice of consumer brands was missing from the legislative equation.

"A lot of us have been working consistently on climate change efforts over the years," she says. "Our consumers are familiar with it, our legislators less so, and we felt that was an important voice."[23]

A collective voice, including that of Nike, resonated again at the 15th United Nations Climate Change Conference (COP15) held in Copenhagen, Denmark, in December 2009. Approximately 40 major companies, led by heavy hitters like Nike, Dow, and Microsoft, sent a letter to President Obama urging him to negotiate a climate deal at the conference.

A portion of the letter follows:

We must put the United States on the path to significant emissions reductions, a stronger economy, and a new position of leadership in the global effort to stabilize our economy. The costs of inaction far outweigh the costs of action. Our environment and economy are at stake. In addition, millions of people in developing and low-lying nations are at risk from climate

and related economic dislocations, which further pose geopolit-
ical threats. These factors highlight the urgency for the Administration to achieve a global deal in the coming days that moves
us ever closer toward a legally-binding agreement that will protect us and future generations.[24]

The result of the conference, which brought together leaders from
around the world, was the Copenhagen Accord. Although met with
mixed reactions, the accord is at least a first step along the onerous
excursion toward a climate change solution.

The accord calls for developed nations to finance a three-year program to the tune of $10 billion per year starting in 2010 to support
projects that will address droughts, floods, and additional impacts of
climate change in developing countries. The document includes an ambitious goal of gathering $100 billion per year by 2020 to address the
climate change issues and to develop clean energy sources in under-
developed countries.

United Nations Secretary-General Ban Ki-moon urged all capable
countries to contribute to the multibillion-dollar fund to help the
poorer countries. He said signing the accord was a good start to tack-
ling climate change and working toward a legally binding treaty in
2010. The accord is merely a political statement and not a legally binding document.

"The faster we have all the signatures, the more momentum we
can give it," said Ki-moon.[25]

U.S. Secretary of State Hillary Clinton is credited with moving the
stalled Copenhagen talks forward after making a surprising announcement about the intentions of the United States. The companies that
participated in sending the letter to Obama urging action at the conference were extremely pleased with the impetus that Clinton gave the
movement.

A portion of the remarks presented by Clinton follows:

> We recognize that an agreement must provide generous finan-
> cial and technological support for developing countries, partic-
> ularly the poorest and most vulnerable, to help them reduce
> emissions and adapt to climate change. That's why we joined
> an effort to mobilize fast-start funding that will ramp up to $10
> billion in 2012 to support the adaptation and mitigation efforts
> of countries in need. In the context of a strong accord in which
> all major economies stand behind mitigation actions and pro-
> vide full transparency as to their implementation, the United
> States is prepared to work with other countries toward a goal
> of jointly mobilizing $100 billion a year by 2020 to address the
> climate change needs of developing countries. We expect this

funding will come from a wide variety of sources, public and private, bilateral and multilateral, including alternative sources of finance. This will include a significant focus on forestry and adaptation, particularly for the poorest and most vulnerable among us.

There should be no doubt about the commitment of the United States to reaching a successful agreement and meeting this great global challenge together. But ultimately, this must be a common effort. It can no longer be about us versus them, this group of nations pitted against that group. We all face this same challenge together.[26]

Clinton noted that China, which has been accused in the past of not fully disclosing specifics about emissions, must be more open with information that affects climate change. Her commitment on behalf of the United States moved the Copenhagen talks off dead-center and led to increased willingness for countries to consider the proposed accord. A subsequent conference was held in Mexico in February 2010 with world leaders working to build on the Copenhagen results.

A month before the Copenhagen conference ended, Nike topped the list on the Third Annual Corporate Climate Scores by receiving 83 out of a possible 100 points. This marked the second consecutive year the company earned top billing on the list, which is compiled by Climate Counts, a nonprofit organization that unites companies and consumers in the fight against global climate change. Climate Counts relies on a scorecard of 22 criteria to gauge corporate climate action in the areas of impact measurement, impact reduction, engagement of public policy related to climate change, and openness and transparency with consumers regarding their corporate activities.

Climate Counts Executive Director Wood Turner believes,

Competition, the most fundamental tenet of a thriving global marketplace, will define the future of corporate climate action and sustainability. Our scores show that companies are motivated to act when they may not measure up to other companies on their response to issues that matter to people. Climate change is certainly one of those issues and companies in every major consumer sector have dialed up their efforts in an evolving economy to make the reduction of global warming pollution a competitive advantage. Our new scores show that many, many companies have begun to take their responsibility for climate action seriously. But the onus is also on consumers. It's time now for them to show business that corporate climate action does not go unnoticed. Companies will continue to see climate protection as an opportunity when consumers tell them in no uncertain terms that inaction is simply not an option.[27]

Inaction is not a word that I have ever seen associated with Nike, which has also been outspoken regarding the issue of deforestation in the Amazon basin. As a result, the company has established a strict policy regarding the use of Brazilian leather in its products. Nike will not use leather produced from cattle raised in the Amazon rainforests. In addition, it requires the suppliers of Brazilian leather to certify in writing that the material they provide is from cattle raised outside the Amazon rainforests.

Having the foresight to implement a stewardship plan so comprehensive that it even includes concern for the Amazon rainforest puts the company in a favorable light with the public. This is the same type of corporate thinking that has amply lined the pockets of Nike executives for decades. The leadership has led to innovative products, association with famous athletes, and ultimately, a big return on investment.

Chapter Nine

The Rich Get Richer

When Nike announces its quarterly fiscal results, financial analysts, competitors, and journalists hold their breath to hear the numbers. The anticipation should have dwindled a long time ago because it really does not matter if Nike loses money or fattens up its coffers. The company will still be a dominant force in the athletic footwear and apparel industry. A dip in sales and the loss of what amounts to just a few dollars now and then for the company is never cause for concern. The release of the earnings is big news in some circles, however, just because the world likes to keep its collective eyes on the big players. Frankly, competitors would like to see the company take a hard tumble from its iconic perch. Although that seems doubtful any time in the near future, competitors keep holding out hope.

Revenue at Nike did slide downward by 4 percent for the fiscal year 2010 second quarter, which ended November 30, 2009. The decrease translated to a drop from the $4.6 billion reported for the same period the year before to $4.4 billion. The company's worldwide futures orders for footwear and apparel—meaning products that were slated to be delivered between December 2009 and April 2010—stood firmly at $7 billion.

Again, as long as the company keeps reporting revenue that starts with a "B," as in billions, I think the future of Nike is secure. The company first reached the billion-dollar milestone way back in 1986, making it unfathomable to conceive how much money the company has earned since then, how much it has paid athletes in endorsement fees, and how wealthy its executives must be.

The second quarter report marked an improvement over the fiscal year 2010 first-quarter results, which showed a 12-percent decrease in revenue to $4.8 billion compared to the $5.4 billion reported for the same period the previous year. The first-quarter results were announced in September 2009. The following month, the Earnings Revenue/Sales Analysis for Textiles, Apparel and Footwear was published by Barclays Capital, the investment banking division of Barclays

Bank. The valuation, compiled by Robert Drbul, managing director and senior equity research analyst with Barclays, provided a bit of foreshadowing that Nike would likely see an improvement in the second quarter.

Drbul's analysis stated:

> While Nike is facing many current challenges, we believe the company is managing through the global turmoil quite well. We continue to believe the shares of Nike are an attractive valuation for long-term investors due to the continued strength of the brand, leading global market positioning, fortress balance sheets, and talented management team. We believe Nike is better positioned given its superior brand strength and is one of the most diversified names from a regional perspective with approximately 60 percent international revenue. We also believe the strength of Nike's balance sheet, with over $3.6 billion in cash and short-term investments, under $500 million of long-term debt, and approximately $7 in net cash per share, gives the company significant financial flexibility to continue to pursue further growth.[1]

Drbul's valuation was right on the money and definitely worth noting because he has been ranked the number one textile, footwear, and apparel analyst in the Institutional Investor's All-America Research Team Survey for six years. He has a wealth of information regarding these industries and companies like Nike. Now, let's turn our attention back to the company's financial results for the second quarter of fiscal year 2010 to see how accurate Drbul was.

Nike officials announced the financial results on December 17, 2009 with the standard conference call and the issuance of a press release. Participating in the call were top financial analysts from Barclays Capital, Goldman Sachs, Citi Investment Research, UBS, Credit Suisse, Bank of America, Susquehanna Financial Group, Sterne Agee, Oppenheimer, and Stifel Nicolaus.

CEO Parker began the conference call by reminding listeners of his projection from the year before:

> It's been about a year ago that I told you Nike would perform well in this challenging economy and expand our lead over our competitors by doing what we do best, and that is delivering superior, innovative products, connecting with our consumers and creating compelling marketing experiences, and operating with discipline and efficiency. As our performance over the last year clearly indicates, we're executing these strategies and winning in the marketplace. We continue to lead the industry in

footwear and apparel product innovation and we're doing that across multiple categories and geographies, and up and down the price spectrum.

Our portfolio of global brands has deepened our personal connections with consumers. We continue to create compelling marketplace experiences with our retail partners, in Nike-owned retail stores and online, and we're managing our business to balance ongoing investments and long-term growth with current profitability and cash flow. Sticking with these principles allows Nike, Inc. to expand competitive separation across multiple dimensions, continue to gain share in key markets around the world, and outperform the industry. Even if revenues dip a bit, our second quarter shows we are able to deliver an appropriate level of financial performance in a rapidly changing environment.[2]

He could have ended the call there or given a brief summary, maybe something like this: "Yes, we lost a small amount of money, but the numbers show we are still at the top of our game." However, he was not quite as succinct and I'm sure everyone listening to the call wanted to hear as much information as possible.

Parker noted that the company has strengthened its brands, maintained profitability for Nike and its retail partners, and positioned itself for accelerated growth by tightly managing the inventory on its books and in the marketplace. He expressed optimism about moving into the second half of fiscal year 2010. He states,

I am very excited about how we're executing against our key growth opportunities. I see a lot of momentum in our direct-to-consumer business, where we continue to deliver positive results, especially online. We are doing a good job of developing our retail capabilities and as I've said many times, that makes us a better wholesale partner and a better company. This really came to life in Tokyo where we opened a new Nike flagship store at Harajuku. It's a great example of how innovative retail experiences really connect with consumers, even in a very tough economy like Japan.

Nike opened its newest store in November 2009 in Tokyo, which is considered the cultural epicenter of Japan. The interior layout of the store was the brainchild of internationally acclaimed designer Masamichi Katayama, who describes the retail facility as having a playground concept "where everyone would feel comfortable experiencing the essence of sports." The store has a unique design that combines Katayama's creativity with the sports innovation of Nike. For example, the chandeliers are designed with 400 pairs of shoes and the walls are made from the soles of 1,600 pairs of shoes.[3]

Is there no end to the amount of inventiveness and money Nike can spend to ensure that each one of its products and stores outclasses the previous one? This particular store, which offers the largest and most extensive line of products among Nike locations in Japan, features sport-specific areas on each floor. The first floor includes a runners' studio, which can provide customers with an analysis of their gait and their running strides.

The second floor houses Japan's largest NikeiD Studio, an interactive area where consumers can actually design original footwear and apparel suitable for their own performance and style needs. If you go up to the third floor, you can visit the Nike Boot Room, where you are greeted by a concierge who is ready to help you select the best products. The new store and the Niketown London facility are the only two retail locations in the world that provide a specialty area for football gear.[4]

Parker points to the Boot Room featured in the Niketown facilities as another example of the retail experiences that keep customers coming back. During his conference call remarks about the fiscal year 2010 second-quarter results, he referenced the company's most recent product innovations and technology. He said the innovations continually enable the company to drive profitable growth across its entire business portfolio.

Looking forward, he said the company still faces significant headwinds in light of the global economic climate and the likelihood that consumers may be a bit more cautious with their spending.

"But given what we all know about the marketplace and about ourselves, we are well positioned to leverage the power of global sports and drive hard against those growth opportunities that have the most impact," Parker said before introducing Charlie Denson, president of the Nike Brand.[5]

One of the most important points made by Denson was that the company's initiative to subsegment the business by category and geography is driving growth via integrated, sharply focused product innovations, retail experiences, and brand connections.

Denson provided examples to demonstrate how the company is focusing on its specific product lines. In basketball, for instance, the focus is on two franchise products—the LeBron VII and the Kobe V shoes—obviously named for LeBron James and Kobe Bryant. He described these products as "pure Nike."

"(The products) use technology and innovation to create a project that defies logic, put it on an incredible athlete that establishes its credibility, and shift the traditional paradigm that says you have to wear a high-top basketball shoe to play at the highest level," explains Denson.[6]

In the area of running, the company created what Denson calls an interconnected consumer experience by staging the Second Annual Human Race; marathons in Chicago, San Francisco, and New York; and a comprehensive Niketown presence in 2009. And, of course, the LunarGlide was the best-selling new shoe of the year.

Regarding soccer, Denson said the company will continually create unprecedented marketing campaigns around the World Cup events and create a new generation of boots that will be touted as "true game-changing technology." Given that one of the most frequently used words when discussing Nike is "technology," it is hard to separate the company from its technology and vice versa.

At the time of the conference call in December, Denson said he was excited about the innovations that would be unveiled within the next nine months. Therefore, some of those products may be launched by the time you read these words. He mentioned the Fresh Air concept of taking Nike Air, the company's famous cushioning system, to the next level of comfort, performance, and appearance. He says,

> We've done a lot of things right to get where we are today and we've got a lot more planned as we move through the second half. I'm very excited and optimistic about this brand, what this brand is capable of doing. I'm not focused on predicting a turnaround. My sites are focused on growing this brand and serving its consumers. I have no doubts that what you see from Nike between now and next fall will show you once again just how connected this brand is to our consumers and our opportunities.[7]

FINANCIAL BREAKDOWN BY GEOGRAPHIC AREAS

Nike's Chief Financial Officer Don Blair also provided earnings information during the conference call. Although the numbers are important for financial analysts who have an interest in them, I will just provide a few points extracted from a transcript of the call.

Blair says,

> While we are seeing hopeful signs of recovery and consumer sentiment around the world, macroeconomic indicators remain mixed and not all of our businesses are recovering at the same pace. Yet, over the last year, we increased our advantage over major competitors and the strength of our diversified portfolio of business enabled us to deliver good financial results. Most important, by continuing to invest in our businesses, while reducing costs and aggressively managing our inventories, we

have positioned ourselves to accelerate growth and profitability as consumer confidence strengthens.[8]

Those words are strikingly similar to the ones used by Parker, so perhaps the same person wrote the copy for each executive to read.

Blair provided a geographic breakdown that includes some interesting tidbits of information. In North America, for example, revenue was down 4 percent for footwear and 6 percent for apparel. The good news is that the decline was almost unnoticeable and certain footwear brands, such as Nike Basketball, Jordan, and Athletic Training, saw an increase in sales. Overall company earnings in North America for the quarter climbed 9 percent to $291 million.

Blair offers his insight regarding the footwear revenue:

While overall industry sales trends have been challenging, we have continued to gain market share in the United States. Results for apparel were also encouraging. As a result of the work we have done to improve the product line, clean up distribution, and manage inventories, the apparel business in North America is much healthier than it's been in some time.[9]

Slight decreases in revenue were experienced in Western Europe, Central and Eastern Europe, Greater China, and Japan, although certain emerging markets saw an 8-percent improvement. Revenue in Western Europe was down 6 percent with an even bigger decrease of 24 percent being reported for Central and Eastern Europe. Blair attributes the declines, in part, to growing unemployment, substantial currency fluctuations, and a decrease in the gross domestic product. South Africa is experiencing an upswing in revenue as interest continues to mount in the soccer craze and the World Cup.

Revenue in Greater China sank 3 percent to $404 million with footwear being down 1 percent, apparel slipping by 7 percent, and equipment decreasing by 2 percent. This is a good place to interject a bit of trivia. Nike started selling shoes in China in 1984 when 200 pairs sold out in less than two weeks at a little shop in Beijing called The Friendship Store. Despite the slight drop in revenue for this particular quarter, China still represents an area of key growth opportunity. For the entire fiscal year 2009, revenue in Greater China increased by 29 percent.

Meanwhile, footwear sales in Japan were up 6 percent in the second quarter, but apparel revenue took a 10-percent fall, resulting in an overall revenue decrease for the quarter of 2 percent. Nike's business in emerging markets delivered strong results with an increase in revenue of 8 percent. "We are seeing improving trends in some geographies, notably China, Western Europe, and the emerging markets," says Blair.[10]

The company has made countless wise business decisions over the years, which explains why it is so powerful in the 21st Century. For example, acquiring Umbro, a top U.K.-based global football brand, helped Nike secure a leadership position in the football industry. In 2002, the company purchased Hurley International, a California-based surf, skate, and snowboard apparel brand. The company saw a 1-percent overall improvement in these other businesses, including Converse, Inc.; Hurley International LLC; Cole Haan; Nike Golf; and Umbro Ltd.

Company officials announced in 2007 that they had reached a deal to sell the Starter brand to Iconix Brand Group, Inc. for $60 million in cash. Two substantial deals were made in 2008, including the sale of Nike Bauer Hockey for $200 million and the acquisition of Umbro for approximately $565 million. The management officials know when to go full speed ahead, but more importantly, when to cut their losses.

MAKING TOUGH DECISIONS

A year earlier on December 17, 2008, the company reported a revenue increase of 6 percent as a result of weak domestic sales being offset by strong revenue in Asia and other foreign markets. While overall revenue in the United States dropped by 1 percent, sales climbed 22 percent in Asia for the quarter. Nike's growing presence on the global stage became distinctly clear in 2003 when international sales exceeded U.S. sales for the first time in the company's history.

Despite apparent growth in Asia and emerging markets throughout the world, the company was forced to make difficult decisions in early 2009 that resulted in a corporate restructuring and downsizing. It's hard to include Nike and downsizing in the same sentence given the company's history and unparalleled growth path. However, Parker blamed the downtrodden economic environment for the company's decision to eliminate approximately 500 of its 35,000 worldwide jobs. The slashed positions were located primarily at the headquarters in Oregon.

"In light of the current economic climate, it is more essential than ever to sharpen our focus on the consumer to maximize opportunities for product innovation and brand management in the marketplace," explains Parker. "The decision to reduce our workforce is a difficult one, but it will put our business in the strongest position possible to continue to deliver long-term profitability and growth."[11]

The workforce reduction was a progression of a corporate realignment the company started in 2007 to bring products to market in a more expeditious manner and to enhance the consumer experience. The strategy called for the company to enhance efficiencies, decrease costs, and reduce management layers. It is unclear what the company has done to reduce management layers, but it is doubtful that it included cutting the pay of top executives. Officials did issue a release saying that the "departing employees will receive a robust and enhanced severance to help support their transition from the company."[12]

Nike's restructuring also included reorganizing the brand into a new model composed of the six geographic areas that were outlined during the conference call, including North America, Western Europe, Eastern and Central Europe, Greater China, Japan, and Emerging Markets. The brand previously had been organized into the four regions of the United States, Asia Pacific, Americas, and Europe/Middle East/Africa. This decision was motivated by a desire to intensify the focus on the company's core business areas, to improve efficiency, and to pay even more attention to connecting with consumers. The new model is intended to enable the company to make quicker decisions by having fewer management layers involved in the process. Information released by the company showed it just shuffled some vice presidents and general managers into different positions.[13]

In a message issued to shareholders shortly after the restructuring was announced, Parker talked about the steps that were necessary to help the company meet the challenges of fiscal year 2009 with laser-like precision. His message in the company's 2009 Annual Report states,

> For many companies, success over the past 12 months was defined as simply surviving. We intend to do more than just survive. We plan to emerge from this downturn competitively stronger. We will do this by delivering appropriate financial performance, while positioning Nike for sustainable, profitable growth over the long term. That means we'll continue to do the things that keep us healthy and opportunistic.

The list cited by Parker as what the company must do to remain healthy did not include downsizing. Rather, the list included the following:

- Delivering compelling products;
- Maintaining the integrity of our brands, while building even stronger relationships with consumers;
- Strengthening and leveraging our operational capability; and
- Creating compelling retail experiences both in our owned retail facilities and with wholesale partners.

Parker promises a continued emphasis on not only domestic markets, but also six foreign markets—namely, Brazil, China, India, Japan,

Russia, and the United Kingdom. The company also will focus on seven key performance and lifestyle categories, including basketball, football, running, action sports, men's training, women's training, and sportswear.

He explains this strategy:

> The category focus helps us connect in really meaningful ways with consumers. Overlay these consumer insights across our key markets and you get a very clear picture of what it takes to deliver relevant products and drive growth into the marketplace. That's our growth strategy. Our job is to do that better than anyone else and I certainly wouldn't bet against us. While we see glimmers of economic recovery, we still have a challenging road ahead. We are well positioned for the future with our fundamentals as strong as they've ever been—deep consumer connections, innovative and compelling products, powerful brands, operational excellence, and a strong balance sheet. We're moving forward with confidence in hand and opportunity in mind.

Nike seems to be as generous with its resources as it is creative with its technology. The list of community outreach projects in which the company plays a role makes it difficult to imagine this is the same business that was once accused of child labor. The company is rapidly becoming well-known for its connection not only with top-name athletes, but also with important causes that are intended to make a positive impact on people's lives.

In the next chapter, we will explore the major causes that are supported by Nike and hear responses from celebrities like Bono, the lead singer of the rock band U2; and renowned cyclist and cancer survivor Lance Armstrong. Even individuals of their stature are pleased that causes important to their heart are receiving a generous hand from Nike.

More companies should look to Nike as an example of how to use their influence in a positive manner to help communities and individuals.

Chapter Ten

Sharing the Wealth

"Nike is an incredible organization not just because of its size and scale, but they do the most incredible ad campaigns. We've all seen them and we've all been moved by them," says Bono, the front man for the popular music group U2. "The idea of having those same creative geniuses working to tell the story of the fight of HIV/AIDS is what this is all about—communicating that the fight is a fight we can all win if we stick together."[1]

Bono said those words in November 2009 when Nike announced a partnership with (RED)™, a groundbreaking initiative co-founded by Bono. The purpose of (RED) is to involve the private sector in increasing awareness and raising money to help the Global Fund eradicate AIDS in Africa. Companies that partner with (RED) agree to donate a percentage of the sales from a particular product to the Global Fund, which gathers resources to prevent and treat AIDS, malaria, and tuberculosis. Statistics provided at the partnership announcement reveal that more than 3,500 men, women, and children die in Sub-Saharan Africa every day, while another 6,000 become newly infected.[2]

The partnership has a twofold purpose of providing funds for educational programs and medication, as well as using the influence of sports figures to engage youths around the world in the fight against this horrible disease. International soccer players who attended the partnership announcement in London included Didier Drogba (Chelsea); Joe Cole (Chelsea); Andrei Arshavin (Arsenal); Marco Materazzi (Inter Milan); Denilson (Arsenal); Lucas Neill (Everton); Clint Dempsey (Fulham); and Seol Ki-Hyeon (Fulham).

"As a global brand and creative company, Nike can play a role in amplifying this important issue," says Parker. "With football as the catalyst, Nike is joining the (RED) movement to fight HIV/AIDS in Africa."[3]

The idea behind the partnership urges customers to "lace up and save lives" by purchasing a pair of Nike red laces. One hundred percent of the sales from the laces will be used to fight AIDS, malaria,

Chelsea soccer player Didier Drogba, left, and Bono
of the rock band U2 participated in the announcement
of a partnership between
Nike and (RED) in London
in late 2009. The partnership is intended to fight
AIDS in Africa. (AP Photo/
Kirsty Wigglesworth)

and tuberculosis. The laces are available at retail locations and at
www.nike.com.

"The fight against AIDS in Africa needs great brands to drive
awareness and engagement," notes Susan Smith Ellis, CEO of (RED).
"Nike is the right partner to connect education with sport and in doing
so, help drive social change, prevention, and understanding of HIV/
AIDS. We are thrilled to have them with us."[4]

Professor Michael Kazatchkine, who serves as executive director of
the Global Fund, believes that wearing the laces can provide a special
bond between the individuals who wear them and the people who are
in need of assistance.

"Wearing these laces is a sign that you care about others and it
helps us to protect and treat millions of people who every day risk
infection or struggle with the effects of HIV," says Kazatchkine.[5]

Numerous videos of Bono and Drogba talking about the partnership are available online. One video I especially like can be found on
www.youtube.com by typing "Bono Teams up with Drogba to Fight
AIDS." In the video, Bono reminds people that just two pills per day
can make all the difference in the world to someone who is at death's
door. In fact, having just this small amount of medication can drastically improve an infected individual's quality of life.

Bono commended the athletes who have agreed to wear the laces
and to spread the word about this important campaign.

"To have these athletes at the peak of their physical fitness think-ing about people who are weak and vulnerable is very poetic, very moving to me," says Bono, who is well-known for his philanthropic endeavors.[6]

Drogba has been drumming up a lot of attention for the campaign by wearing his laces when he competes. "This is a bigger fight than winning games. Saving lives is very important," says the footballer on the YouTube video.[7]

Nike's connection with another athlete, cyclist Lance Armstrong, has resulted in a full-blown global initiative to battle another disease—cancer.

MAKING A DIFFERENCE IN THE FIGHT AGAINST CANCER

Many people understand the horror of cancer and have seen first-hand how this disease can rapidly devastate a body and steal life from its victims. Nike and the Lance Armstrong Foundation have made this subject a priority each year as they continue to raise millions of dollars to conduct research and raise awareness.

Nike, which has been partnering with the Lance Armstrong Foundation since 2004, created the LIVESTRONG wristband. To date, more than 70 million bands have been worn as part of a global phe-nomenon through which increasing numbers of people are becoming aware of the need to be aggressive in the fight against this vicious dis-ease. More recently, Nike developed a LIVESTRONG collection of run-ning and training footwear, apparel, and accessories.

In June 2009, the company began a grassroots marketing campaign featuring Armstrong, other top-notch athletes, celebrities, and survi-vors who joined together in the worldwide fight against cancer. The campaign, called "It's About You," includes a television commercial, videos of people telling inspirational cancer stories, social networking components to engage viewers, and various LIVESTRONG events throughout the United States and in France.

"The campaign is not about me. I'm just one person and I can't fight a global epidemic alone," says Armstrong, a cancer survivor and seven-time Tour de France winner. "We're celebrating the strength of those facing the adversity of cancer and giving them new ways to share their stories. It's about inspiring people to turn hope into action, so we can beat this disease that strikes far too many, too often."[8]

Nike compiled a digital collection of short films that feature stories from cancer survivors and individuals who have been touched by someone living with cancer. Athletes who told their stories included Boston Red Sox pitcher Jon Lester, as well as sprinters Sanya Richards and LaShawn Merritt. Others featured on the films were actors Patrick Dempsey and Evan Handler, and other cancer survivors including

Lance Armstrong leads the Astana Team during the first stage of the Giro d'Italia Tour of Italy cycling race in May 2009. (AP Photo/ Marco Trovati, File)

three-time Iditarod winner Lance Mackey and Sean Swarner, who earned the title of the first cancer survivor to reach the peak of Mount Everest.

"Lance is a symbol of hope and courage for people living with this terrible disease," notes Scott MacEachern, Nike general manager for LIVESTRONG. "We are encouraging people to actively join the fight against cancer and giving them innovative ways to spread that message to others."[9]

Information about the campaign is available at www.LIVESTRONG. org and www.nike.com. Nike is providing social media tools to enable individuals to share their messages of hope and to encourage others to join the global initiative. Individuals who visited the Nike site in 2009 were able to submit inspirational messages online or by text to a custom-made chalkbot that then wrote the messages in yellow chalk on the roads of the Tour de France. This is in line with the Tour's tradition of having inspirational messages written along the course route. Participating individuals received an email message giving them the Global Positioning System coordinates of the location where their message was written. Event images can be viewed on the Nike Web site. The company is likely to repeat the same or a similar social media extravaganza in the coming years.

The company also teamed with the Lance Armstrong Foundation to present "Stages," a spectacular global art exhibit and sale to raise funds for cancer research. The exhibit, showcasing the works of the world's most accomplished and up-and-coming artists, opened at the renowned Galerie Emmanuel Perrotin in Paris in July 2009 and later traveled to the United States.

"We're taking the LIVESTRONG message, which is already in the global lexicon, and giving it a different type of energy and voice," explains Parker. "At the same time, we're combining the fight against cancer with sports and art to create a larger community that is aware and engaged in the fight against cancer."[10]

Nike officials say the "Stages" event unites the worlds of art, sports, and philanthropy in a celebration of the human potential inspired by Armstrong and dedicated to the ongoing fight.

"It will project hope, strength, and commitment to millions and carry the LIVESTRONG Global Cancer Campaign all over the world," says Armstrong. "I am humbled by the effort and energy given by so many to bring Stages to life."[11]

Artists who contributed to the 2009 show were Cai Guo-Qiang, Rosson Crow, Jules De Balincourt, Shepard Fairey, KAWS, Andreas Gursky, Geoff McFetridge, Catherine Opie, Yoshitomo Nara, Jose Parla, Raymond Pettibon, Lara Pittman, Richard Prince, Ed Ruscha, Tom Sachs, Kenny Scharf, Aaron Young, Eric White, and Christopher Wool.

Raising funds to battle diseases is not the only charitable act in which Nike participates. It also expends energy, time, and money to empower youths.

LENDING A HELPING HAND TO KIDS

Nike is downright bold, almost to the point of being brazen, when it comes to promoting its products. However, the company exercises decorum and more self-restraint when it comes to publicizing its good deeds. In fact, most of the information about money it donates and programs it undertakes to help children is available on the company Web site, but I have not seen much publicity elsewhere. The company is making a difference without ruthless self-promotion.

Last year, Nike joined forces with the Doernbecher Children's Hospital in Oregon to empower children by letting them help design footwear. This marked the sixth year that the company and hospital united to design the Doernbecher Freestyle footwear collection, a project that pairs patients with Nike designers to create shoes that depict the children's personal stories.

The children help design the shoes by expressing their creativity with assistance from Nike designers throughout the entire process from choosing a shoe style to picking out materials, colors, patterns, and other specific details. The shoes are then sold to raise money for the hospital, which is part of the Oregon Health and Science University. More than $2 million has been raised from the sale of the shoes during the six-year project.[12]

"We are proud to support this one-of-a-kind project," says Elliott Hill, vice president of global retail for Nike. "Doernbecher Freestyle is about empowerment through design, bringing together bright young patients and some of our most talented Nike designers to give back to Doernbecher Children's Hospital."[13]

The shoes, designed with assistance from patients ranging in age from 11 to 14, can be purchased at www.nike.com or at select retail locations. Prices start at $88.

Sue Nicol, executive director of the Doernbecher Foundation, expresses gratitude for the financial impact that Nike has made. More importantly though, she stresses the priceless experience the company is providing for the ill children. "Their moment in the spotlight as a Nike shoe designer is one they'll never forget," she says.[14]

Other Nike efforts to help children include the annual 5K for Kids Run in Waikiki, Hawaii, and the Back Your Block program. The 5K event, which has been hosted by the company for the past 10 years, raises money to support the athletic programs and to purchase playground equipment for the Oahu schools.

Back Your Block is a national grant program aimed at supporting school and community groups that offer sports programs. The $650,000 grant initiative was started in 2009 with each of Nike's 175 U.S. retail locations participating.

"This represents an excellent opportunity for us to be involved in local communities," says Kari Mitchell, senior manager for Nike retail community relations. "We are excited to offer a program where anyone can nominate their favorite organization for a grant and vote on the applicants they feel most passionate about."[15]

More information is available for organizations and nonprofit community and school groups at www.nikebackyourblock.com.

Nike has transitioned its corporate giving to an online grant application process and no longer accepts hard copy or email proposals for its various donation programs. The company reviews requests for product donations, but it does not accept unsolicited appeals for cash assistance. Further information about applying for various programs is available at www.nikebiz.com. It is worth noting that the company does not provide charitable support for individuals; individual sports team sponsorships; for-profit ventures; religious groups for religious purposes; lobbying, political, or fraternal activities; individual study, research, or travel grants; capital campaigns, endowment funds or memorials; awards that require the company or its employees to raise money on behalf of the organization bestowing the award; and unsolicited auction product or table sponsorships.

TAKING IT GLOBAL

Teaching boys and girls the importance of gender equality took center stage for Nike's community outreach at the beginning of 2009. Parker served as a panelist for a session, entitled "The Girl Effect on Development," at the World Economic Forum's Annual Meeting in Switzerland in January. Information can be found by viewing www.girleffect.org.

Parker notes that including the "girl effect" on the agenda signals a turning point in understanding the potential contribution that adolescent girls can make to their own communities and to the overall global economy.

"When given an opportunity to participate, girls are a powerful force for social and economic change," he reminds everyone. "That's exactly what we need right now."[16]

Parker was in good company on the panel with Melinda French Gates, co-chair of the Bill & Melinda Gates Foundation; Ngozi Okonjo-Iweala, managing director of World Bank; Mari Pangestu, minister of trade for Indonesia; Ann Veneman, executive director of the United Nations' Children's Fund; and Muhammad Yunus, managing director of the Grameen Bank and board member of the United Nations Foundation.

Parker might stand out as an unlikely choice for such a panel of guests until you realize that the Nike Foundation spearheaded the creation of www.girleffect.org with collaboration from the NoVo Foundation, the United Nations Foundation, and the Coalition for Adolescent Girls. The Nike Foundation is a nonprofit organization created to focus on investing in adolescent girls as a driving force for change in developing countries.

Nike points out startling examples on its Web site to show why more attention must be focused on helping these young girls. In a press release announcing the World Economic Forum, Nike mentions the following:

> In India, for example, adolescent pregnancy results in nearly $100 billion in lost potential income over a lifetime. That's equal to the world's total humanitarian assistance over the last 17 years combined. However, innovative organizations like Going to School are showing girls in India a world of possibilities beyond early marriage and early child-bearing. The "Be an Entrepreneur Fund" inspires girls to create businesses that solve the social, economic, and environmental problems they face in their daily lives. With little more than one half a cent of every international development dollar going to girls, there is a desperate and immediate need to increase funding to programs

that unleash the girl effect and enable girls to achieve their potential.[17]

Panel participants believe that reaching girls at an adolescent age is vital to ensuring they are not subjected to issues, such as early marriage and pregnancy, which could interfere with a successful future.

"We'll never be able to achieve the United Nations Millennium Development Goal of eradicating extreme poverty, if we do not address the issues girls face," says Okonjo-Iweala of the World Bank. "Directing resources to address gender equity, universal education, child and maternal health is a start, but the success of reaching every goal is dependent on the critical well-being, safety, and participation of the world's girls."[18]

These theories uphold what Kelley Skoloda has been saying throughout this book about women becoming a dominant force that marketers must target. It makes sense that if we reach more girls, it will increase the overall purchasing power of the female audience as these girls reach adulthood.

A few months after the World Economic Forum's Annual Meeting, officials from the Nike Foundation participated in a "Global Symposium on Engaging Men and Boys in Achieving Gender Equality" in Rio de Janeiro, Brazil. The goal of the event was to discuss best practices relevant to teaching men and boys the urgency of reducing violence against women and girls, promoting sexual and reproductive health, preventing and treating HIV/AIDS, and stressing the importance of proper fatherhood and care-giving.

Lisa MacCallum, managing director of the Nike Foundation, stresses,

> The girl effect is about breaking the cycle of poverty and building a sustainable global economy. Girls and boys are equally critical to the solution. The programs we're funding create opportunities for men and boys to see how whole communities benefit when girls are seen as powerful economic actors and family resource managers, rather than a resource drain and financial burden.[19]

RANDOM ACTS OF KINDNESS

Following are a number of other actions that Nike has taken over the years that fall into the category of community outreach:

- 1999: Knight establishes the Bowerman Track Renovation Program in honor of his Nike co-founder and friend. The money is used to revamp track and field facilities used by youths around the world.

- 2001: After the terrorist attacks on September 11, 2001, a group of 265 Nike employees run a seven-week relay to raise money for the families of the victims. The Run Across America relay began in Astoria, Oregon, and included stops at 44 firehouses before ending in New York.
- 2002: As part of its 30th anniversary celebration, Nike restores approximately 90 outdoor basketball courts in Portland, Oregon.
- 2002: The company starts a national community program called NikeGo to promote physical activity among youths.
- 2008: Nike launches the first Human Race, the world's largest running event with more than 750,000 participants. The goal is to celebrate the sport of running and to connect runners through a physical and virtual event.

Nike has partnered with the World Wildlife Fund to make the Human Race more environmentally friendly. In particular, the company tries to reduce the amount of printed materials, encourages carpooling and the use of public transportation to and from the event, and maximizes the recycling and composting of waste generated at the race locations.

Parker was not available to answer questions about why community outreach is so important to Nike. However, the company continues to spend some of its profits to help others. Just as Nike has made an impact on sports, cultures around the globe, advertising, and the lives of children, it is also poised to make an equally significant impact on community outreach efforts.

Chapter Eleven

There Is No Finish Line

Although my book is coming to a close, the story of Nike will never be complete. The company must be on its toes every minute because it is constantly unveiling a new product, launching another advertising campaign, supporting sponsored athletes, being visible in the community, or tinkering with new technology. The work never ends and that's a good thing for the company, the athletes, the consumers, and the people who are helped by the outreach programs.

The company closed 2009 by announcing a new addition to the Zoom Kobe series of shoes that will be available this year. The announcement coincided with the company's forward-thinking philosophy of always trying to outsmart its competitors by being the first to bring new products to the market.

Kobe Bryant, star player for the Los Angeles Lakers, joined the company in unveiling the Nike Zoom Kobe V, hailed as the lightest basketball shoe to date. Bryant had challenged company designers to make his signature footwear lighter and lower than the Kobe IV, which he debuted during the 2008–2009 championship season. The designers met the challenge by delivering a shoe that weighs only 10.6 ounces, which is one ounce lighter than the previous version.

"I wanted to push the envelope with a shoe that meets the demands of my style of play," says Bryant. "The Kobe V is lighter, lower, and more stable. Nike has done it again."[1]

It seems appropriate to include the new Bryant shoe in this chapter since he describes it as another example where the company has "done it again." I am confident the company will do it over and over again in 2010 and beyond in terms of creating state-of-the-art products.

Bryant's vision for the new shoe came not from the basketball court, but from the soccer field.

"I watch a lot of soccer and have seen how the best footballers in the world make sharp cuts at top speed in lightweight, low-cut footwear," says Bryant. "The demands they make on their feet and ankles aren't that different from what I'm doing on the court, yet nobody assumes they should play in high tops."[2]

In order to create a shoe that met Bryant's request, the Nike Sports Research Lab conducted hundreds of hours of testing to develop the low-top footwear without compromising stability. The result of the research and testing was a shoe with a modified medial arch and sculpted external heel counter that moves with the foot and facilitates multidirectional cutting.

Matt Nurse, senior researcher with the Sports Research Lab, explains,

> The journey from a high-top to a low-top basketball shoe is far more complex than simply cutting off the ankle collar as we demonstrated with the Nike Zoom Kobe IV. With the Kobe V, we constructed an even lighter-weight support system that provides superior, one-to-one lockdown while moving with the foot, not against it.[3]

Nike is accustomed to designing products that move with the flow of its athletes. This acquiescent concept is somewhat contrary to the philosophy of the company leaders who tend to resist the ordinary and confront controversy by forging new pathways in the sportswear industry. Then again, it all goes back to catering to their athletes. The company's product line is as diverse and colorful as the executives at the helm.

I was not able to include all of the additional products announced in 2009 because it was more imperative to provide a comprehensive overview of the company's origins, innovations, leadership ideals, and milestones. The rock-solid business principles and devoted leadership that we have explored have positioned the company for continued success.

The biographical sketches listed on Nike's Web site about its key executives do not do justice to the company's leaders. For example, Knight is described as the chairman of the board of directors in a brief paragraph that reads:

> Mr. Knight is a co-founder of the company and, except for the period from June 1983 through September 1984, served as its president from 1968 to 1990, and from June 2000 to 2004. Prior to 1968, Mr. Knight was a certified public accountant with Price Waterhouse and Coopers & Lybrand and was an assistant professor of business administration at Portland State University.[4]

After everything I have learned about the company and the men behind it, I know the description does not adequately portray Knight's impact on the business. However, consumers buying the products and

The co-founders of Nike share a laugh as Bill Bowerman, left, is presented with an award at Hayward Field from Phil Knight in 1999. (AP Photo/John Gress)

the people reflecting on the advertising campaigns may not care about the people behind the company. They may not want or need to know about the relentless dedication and the years of exhausting work that Knight and Bowerman poured into their company. Instead, they probably only care about the products, and that's just fine with Nike because the men behind the vision wanted nothing more than for people to buy their shoes, apparel, accessories, and equipment.

"To understand Nike, you have to look at where we came from and where we are going," says Parker, who is well qualified to continue leading the company into tomorrow. He has a long history with the company, coming onboard as one of its first footwear designers in 1979. He has served in a variety of pivotal leadership roles and has been a driving force behind many of the company's innovations.

During his long tenure at the company, Parker obviously got to know the founders extremely well. He describes the collaboration between Knight and Bowerman as "a perfect match," especially since both men were brilliant and pig-headed, qualities that worked well for them throughout their careers. They achieved a remarkable dream that has touched millions of lives going all the way back to that auspicious day when they met for the first time at Hayward Field at the University of Oregon. Incidentally, the field was named for Bill Hayward, the first track director at the University of Oregon. He preceded Bowerman and served in the position from 1904 to 1947.

Bowerman became head track coach in 1948 and remained in the position until 1973. He was able to witness the reality of his vision and enjoy the success of his company for decades before passing away on Christmas Eve in 1999. His dream will continue to thrive.

Parker summarizes the thrust behind Nike's success with these words:

> There are many reasons for Nike's survival. A passion for sports was key as was a deep knowledge of the needs of athletes. Luck played a role, too, but I have my own theory. I believe the most overwhelming connection between (Knight and Bowerman) was their shared belief in human potential, the belief that we are all capable of more . . . the bright light that connects those early days at Hayward Field to the Nike of today.
>
> We've seen the light shine in the face of athletes around the world, athletes who show us not how to do what they do, but how to live as they live—committed to self and team, willing to do the hard work that is required to excel and ready to stand up for what we believe in.
>
> Staying true to our nature at Nike also means embracing change. These changes mean more opportunities for Nike to lead and do what we do best—connect deeply with athletes and gain insights that translate into the best products in the world. Nike is a reflection of the people who started this company and the people who continue to move this company forward and we all believe the same thing. There is no finish line.[5]

Notes

CHAPTER 1

1. Deion Sanders Biography, http://deion-sanders.com/bio.html (accessed November 20, 2009).
2. Nike, "AIR JORDAN: History of the Franchise," http://www.nike.com/jumpman23/#/history (accessed October 8, 2009).
3. Nike, "Jordan Brand Launches the AIR JORDAN 2010," news release, November 11, 2009.

CHAPTER 2

1. Nike, "History and Heritage: When Nike Breathed Its First Breath," http://www.nikebiz.com/company_overview/history/1950s.html (accessed March 23, 2009).
2. Ibid.
3. Nike, "History and Heritage: The Nike Brand and Company," http://www.nikebiz.com/company_overview/history/1970s.html (accessed March 23, 2009).
4. Bob Welch, "Here's the Woman behind Swoosh," *The Register-Guard*, March 3, 2002.
5. Ibid.
6. Nike, "History and Heritage: The Nike Brand and Company," http://www.nikebiz.com/company_overview/history/1970s.html (accessed March 23, 2009).
7. Nike, "History and Heritage," http://www.nikebiz.com/company_overview/history/1980s.html (accessed March 23, 2009).
8. Ibid.
9. Ibid.

CHAPTER 3

1. Nike, "Nike Creates Men vs. Women Virtual Running Race," news release, March 2009.
2. Ibid.

3. Nike, "20,000 Women from around the World Take Part in Sixth Annual Nike Women's Marathon," news release, October 18, 2009.

4. Ibid.

5. Ibid.

6. Nike, "Diversity and Inclusion," http://www.nikebiz.com/company.overview/diversity (accessed July 12, 2009).

7. Altimeter Group, ENGAGEMENTdb Report, July 2009, http://www.engagementdb.com (accessed September 2, 2009).

8. Wetpaint, "New Study Indicates Social Media Pays," news release, July 20, 2009.

9. Nike, "Nike Introduces New Nike+ SportBand and Enhanced Digital Running Destination," news release, July 13, 2009.

10. "The World's Most Innovative Companies," *Fast Company*, www.fastcompany.com/magazine/123/the-worlds-most-innovative-companies.html (accessed October 11, 2009).

11. Newt Barrett and Joe Pulizzi, *Get Content Get Customers* (New York: McGraw-Hill, 2009).

12. "China Bans Nike TV Ad as National Insult," *China Daily*, December 7, 2004, http://www.chinadaily.com (accessed December 23, 2009).

13. Nike, "LeBron James Heads to London," news release, September 2, 2009.

14. Jeremy Mullman, "Jordan Brand: An American Hottest Brand Case Study," *Advertising Age*, November 16, 2009.

CHAPTER 4

1. "Jordan Enters with Robinson, Stockton," *Associated Press*, September 11, 2009.

2. Ibid.

3. Nike, "Jordan Brand Welcomes Dwyane Wade," news release, July 17, 2009.

4. Ibid.

5. Nike, "Jordan Branch Launches AIR JORDAN 2010," news release, November 11, 2009.

6. Nike, "Jordan Brand Goes Beyond XX3 to Unveil the Future of the Brand," news release, January 8, 2009.

7. Nike, "Jordan Brand and Chris Paul Take over New Orleans to Celebrate Launch of Paul's Next Signature Shoe," news release, March 4, 2009.

8. Ibid.

9. Nike, "Jordan Brand Launches the AIR JORDAN XX3: Celebrating 23 Years of a Legacy," news release, January 1, 2008.

10. Nike, "Jordan Brand's Educational Grant Program Opens Grant Cycle for 2009–2010 School Year," news release, February 18, 2009.

11. Nike, "Jordan Brand Awards $1 Million to the Pursuit of Educational Excellence," news release, December 11, 2009.

12. Nike, "Jordan Brand and All-Star Dwyane Wade Give Back to Miami Norland Senior High School," news release, November 12, 2009.

13. Ibid.

14. Nike, "Team Jordan," www.Jumpman23.com (accessed October 15, 2009).

15. Nike, "SRC Universal Motown Recording Artist Akon to Perform at 2009 Jordan Classic," news release, April 10, 2009.

16. Darren Rovell, "Michael Jordan's Son Not Free to Wear AIR JORDANs," CNBC Sports, October 20, 2009.

17. Antonio Gonzalez, "Marcus Jordan Wears Dad's Shoes, Blows School's $3-Million Adidas Deal," *Huffington Post*, November 4, 2009.

CHAPTER 5

1. Matt Markey, "Buckeyes Sport Retro Look of 1954," *Toledo Blade*, November 18, 2009.

2. Coachtressel.com, "Title Tribute to 1954 Team," http://www.coachtressel.com/news/viewArticle.php?Article=795 (accessed December 2, 2009).

3. Coachtressel.com, "Special New Uniforms," www.coachtressel.com/news/viewArticle.php?Article=770 (accessed December 2, 2009).

4. Matt Markey, "Buckeyes Sport Retro Look of 1954," *Toledo Blade*, November 18, 2009.

5. Nike, "Nike Outfits NCAA Basketball Teams for Battle with Innovative Uniform Systems," news release, March 10, 2009.

6. Ibid.

7. Ibid.

8. Paul Levitan, "Redeem Team Brings Back U.S. Basketball Glory," *News Blaze*, October 24, 2008.

9. Nike, "Nike Debuts the Ultimate in Performance Protection," news release, January 7, 2009.

10. "Nike Kicks Off Football Season with Prepare for Combat," *New York Times*, September 11, 2009.

11. Ibid.

12. Ibid.

CHAPTER 6

1. "Nike Says It Stands by Tiger Woods," *Market Watch*, December 2, 2009, http://www.marketwatch.com (accessed December 8, 2009).

2. TAG Heuer, "TAG Heuer Stands by Brand Ambassador," news release, December 9, 2009.

3. "Gillette, Accenture Drop Tiger Woods," *Cincinnati Business Journal*, December 14, 2009.

4. "AT&T Terminates Sponsorship of Scandal-Hit Tiger Woods," *Business World*, January 3, 2010.

5. "Woods Voted PGA Tour Player of the Year by Peers," *Reuters*, December 19, 2009, http://www.reuters.com/assets (accessed December 20, 2009).

6. Greg Stoda, "Tiger Woods Will Be Welcomed Back to Golf When It's Right," *Palm Beach Post*, December 17, 2009.

7. PGA Tour, "Nicklaus Weighs in on Woods' Major Quest," news release, January 8, 2010.

8. Nike, "Nike Golf Kicks off Commercial Celebrating Tiger Woods' Return," news release, February 23, 2009.

9. Ibid.

10. Ibid.

11. Lisa DiCarlo, "With Tiger Woods, It's Nike, Nike Everywhere," *Forbes*, July 8, 2009.

12. Ibid.

13. Liz Clarke, "S. Williams Is Fined $82,500," *Washington Post*, December 1, 2009.

14. Ibid.

15. SportsOneSource.com, "Nike Backs Serena Williams," September 14, 2009, www.sportsonesource.com/news/spor/spor_article.asp?section=88Prod= 1&id=29646 (accessed October 19, 2009).

16. Ibid.

17. Nike, "Nike Statement Regarding Michael Vick," news release, July 19, 2007.

18. ESPN.com, "Vick, Eagles Agree to Two-Year Deal," news release, August 13, 2009.

19. Ibid.

20. Ibid.

21. Ibid.

22. ESPN.com, "Nike, Vick Do Not Have Agreement," news release, October 1, 2009.

23. Ibid.

24. Ibid.

CHAPTER 7

1. Nike, "Nike Combines Boot Technology with Digital Training Program to Create Total Game Improvement Package," news release, December 10, 2009.

2. Ibid.

3. Nike, "Steve Nash Continues Commitment to Sustainability with Nike Zoom MVP Trash Talk," news release, April 16, 2009.

4. Ibid.

5. Ibid.

6. Nike, "History and Heritage," http://www.nikebiz.com/company_ overview/history (accessed April 22, 2009).

7. Nike, "Nike's Considered Design Products," http://www.nikebiz.com/ responsibility/considered_design/features/ (accessed October 3, 2009).

8. Ibid.

9. Nike, "History and Heritage," http://www.nikebiz.com/company_ overview/history (accessed October 3, 2009).

10. "ASTRO Studios Wins Design of the Decade Awards from World's Most Prestigious Design Competition," *Business Wire*, November 22, 1999, http://www.thefreelibrary.com/ASTRO+Studios+Wins+%60Design+of_The+ Decade+A (accessed October 6, 2009).

11. Ibid.

12. Ibid.

13. Nike, "Lunarlite Foam Technology," http://www.nikemedia.com/en/technology/lunarlite_foam_technology (accessed August 3, 2009).

14. Greg Bishop, "What's In a Shoe?" *New York Times*, August 30, 2009.

15. Nike, "Nike Swift Apparel," http://www.nikemedia.com/en/technology/nike_swift (accessed August 3, 2009).

16. Nike, "PreCool Technology," http://www.nikemedia.com/en/technology/precool_technology (accessed August 3, 2009).

17. Cliff Kuang, "The Next Big Step in Running Shoes?" *Fast Company*, December 23, 2009.

18. Nike, "Flywire," http://www.nikemedia.com/en/technology/flywire (accessed August 3, 2009).

19. Nike, "Nike Golf Creates Transformational New Driver for Golfers," news release, December 15, 2008.

20. Bill Pennington, "Golfers Have Clothes Laid out for Them," *New York Times*, July 12, 2009.

21. "Nike Introduces U.S. Open Competition Looks for Serena Williams, Roger Federer, Rafael Nadal and Maria Sharapova," *New York Times*, August 26, 2009.

22. Ibid.

23. Nike, "Nike and USOC Unveil U.S. Olympic and Paralympic Team Look," news release, November 4, 2009.

24. Ibid.

CHAPTER 8

1. Nike, "Innovate for a Better World," http://www.nikebiz.com/responsibility/cr_governance.html (accessed June 7, 2009).

2. Ibid.

3. "100 Best Corporate Citizens," *Corporate Responsibility Officer*, www.thecro.com/100best09 (accessed November 5, 2009).

4. Ethisphere, "2009 World's Most Ethical Companies," http://ethisphere.com/about/ (accessed November 5, 2009).

5. "100 Best Companies to Work For," *Fortune*, http://money.cnn.com/magazines/fortune/bestcompanies/2008/snapshots/82.html (accessed November 5, 2009).

6. "Nike Chairman Phil Knight with Michael Moore," www.youtube.com (accessed November 12, 2009).

7. Nike, "History and Heritage," http://www.nikebiz.com/company_overview/history (accessed October 3, 2009).

8. Nike, "Uzbekistan Cotton Production," http://www.nikebiz.com/responsibility/considered_design/features/2009_Uzbekistancott (accessed on October 4, 2009).

9. Nike, "Letter from Hannah Jones," http://www.nikebiz.com/responsibility/documents/_NikeSustainableBusinessInnovationle (accessed October 29, 2009).

10. Nike, "Nike Helps Contract Factories Reduce Climate Footprint," http://www.nikebiz.com/responsibility/considered_design/features/greener_contract_fact (accessed October 29, 2009).

11. "Green Rankings 2009," *NEWSWEEK*, September 16, 2009.

12. Ibid.

13. Nike, "Global 100 Most Sustainable Corporations Announced," news release, January 28, 2009.

14. Ibid.

15. Nike, "PopTech Launches New Signature Offering," news release, October 22, 2009.

16. Ibid.

17. Nike, "Nike & Creative Commons Create a System for Open Innovation," news release, February 10, 2009.

18. Nike, "Nike Goes to Washington," http://www.nikebiz.com/responsibility/considered_design/features/sustainability_effort (accessed September 12, 2009).

19. Nike, "Nike Urges U.S. Senate to Address Climate Issues," http://www.nikebiz.com/resonsibility/considered_design/features/addressing_climate (accessed September 15, 2009).

20. U.S. Chamber of Commerce, "Donohue Comments on Climate Change," news release, September 29, 2009.

21. Nike, "Nike Statement Regarding U.S. Chamber of Commerce," news release, September 30, 2009.

22. Nike, "Nike & BICEP Partner to Work on Climate Change and Energy Issues," http://www.nikebiz.com/responsibility/considered_design/index.html (accessed October 27, 2009).

23. Ibid.

24. Glenn Thrush, "Microsoft, Nike, Dow Urge Obama to Seal Copenhagen Deal," December 15, 2009, www.politico.com/blogs (accessed January 1, 2010).

25. "UN Urges Countries to Sign Climate Accord," *Associated Press*, December 22, 2009.

26. Hillary Clinton, "Remarks at the United Nations Framework Convention on Climate Change," U.S. Department of State, December 17, 2009.

27. Climate Counts, "Third Annual Climate Counts Scores Show Economic Downturn Doesn't Detract from Corporate Commitment," news release, November 18, 2009.

CHAPTER 9

1. Robert Drbul, Barclays Capital, October 19, 2009.

2. Nike, "Nike, Inc. Reports Fiscal 2010 Second Quarter Results," news release, December 17, 2009.

3. Nike, "Nike Opens Premiere Flagship Store in Tokyo, Japan," news release, November 12, 2009.

4. Ibid.

5. Nike, "Nike, Inc. Reports Fiscal 2010 Second Quarter Results," news release, December 17, 2009.

6. Ibid.

7. Ibid.

8. Ibid.

9. Ibid.

10. Ibid.

11. Nike, "Nike, Inc. Restructuring Statement," news release, May 14, 2009.

12. Ibid.

13. Nike, "Nike, Inc. Announces Nike Brand Geographical Restructuring to Enhance Consumer Focus," news release, March 20, 2009.

CHAPTER 10

1. "Bono Teams up with Drogba to Fight AIDS," www.youtube.com (accessed December 1, 2009).

2. Nike, "Nike & (RED) Unite to Leverage the Power of Sport to Fight HIV/AIDS," news release, November 30, 2009.

3. Ibid.

4. Ibid.

5. Ibid.

6. "Bono Teams up with Drogba to Fight AIDS," www.youtube.com (accessed December 1, 2009).

7. Ibid.

8. Nike, "Nike and Lance Armstrong Unite to Inspire and Mobilize the World in the Fight Against Cancer," news release, June 26, 2009.

9. Ibid.

10. Nike, "Lance Armstrong and Nike Launch Stages," news release, July 16, 2009.

11. Ibid.

12. Nike, "Nike and Doernbecher Children's Hospital Collaborate to Empower Kids Through Design," news release, November 12, 2009.

13. Ibid.

14. Ibid.

15. Nike, "Nike Announces $650,000 Back Your Block National Grant Program," news release, June 30, 2009.

16. Nike, "World Economic Forum Gives Adolescent Girls a Voice on the Global Stage," news release, January 30, 2009.

17. Ibid.

18. Ibid.

19. Nike, "Nike Foundation Joins Cross Sector Leaders in First-of-its-kind Symposium," news release, March 30, 2009.

CHAPTER 11

1. Nike, "Nike and Kobe Bryant Launch New Zoom Kobe V," news release, December 29, 2009.

2. Ibid.

3. Ibid.

4. Nike, "Behind a Great Company are Strong Leaders," http://www.nikebiz.com/company_overview/executives (accessed July 23, 2009).

5. Nike, "History and Heritage," http://nikebiz.com/media (accessed July 24, 2009).

Index

About the Author

TRACY CARBASHO is an award-winning journalist who has been recognized for her investigative reporting skills. After working as a journalist, editor, and columnist for a daily newspaper in West Virginia for 13 years, she began a full-time freelance writing career in 2000. She has written for business publications and legal journals throughout the United States.

She is a sought-after contributor to magazines, newspapers, and trade publications, especially for articles that require extensive research, investigative know-how, a quick turnaround, and detailed analysis. In addition to being passionate about writing, she also has a knack for editing and is well regarded for her knowledge of *The Chicago Manual of Style*. She recently edited *Too Busy to Shop*, a book about marketing to busy women, and *Fatness to Fitness*, which provides a wealth of health-related information.

Writing has always been a saving grace for Carbasho, who has also worked as the communications director for a steelworkers' union and the public relations coordinator for a college. Her proudest moment, however, occurred in 2003 when the West Virginia Legislature approved the Groucho Act, a state bill named in memory of her beloved dog. She single-handedly lobbied for two years to gain support for the state legislation, which made animal cruelty a felony. Her relentless efforts to get the bill passed proved that one person can make a difference in the world.

Today, Carbasho lives in West Virginia with her best friend, Mojo. She is currently writing a series of books about the adventures of Groucho and Mojo. In addition to her love for animals and her zest for writing, she is a Martin Luther King Jr. historian and is skilled in self-defense.